John Smith Futhey

Historical discourse delivered on the occasion of the one hundred and fiftieth anniversary of the Upper Octorara Presbyterian Church : Chester County, Pennsylvania, September 14, 1870

John Smith Futhey

Historical discourse delivered on the occasion of the one hundred and fiftieth anniversary of the Upper Octorara Presbyterian Church : Chester County, Pennsylvania, September 14, 1870

ISBN/EAN: 9783337263089

Printed in Europe, USA, Canada, Australia, Japan

Cover: Foto ©ninafisch / pixelio.de

More available books at **www.hansebooks.com**

HISTORY

OF

UPPER OCTORARA CHURCH.

1720—1870.

UPPER OCTORARA CHURCH, ERECTED IN 1840.

HISTORICAL DISCOURSE

DELIVERED ON THE OCCASION OF THE

ONE HUNDRED AND FIFTIETH ANNIVERSARY

OF THE

Upper Octorara Presbyterian Church,

CHESTER COUNTY, PENNSYLVANIA.

SEPTEMBER 14, 1870.

By J. SMITH FUTHEY, Esq.

WITH AN ACCOUNT OF THE CELEBRATION AND AN APPENDIX.

PHILADELPHIA:
HENRY B. ASHMEAD, BOOK AND JOB PRINTER,
Nos. 1102 AND 1104 SANSOM STREET.
1870.

TABLE OF CONTENTS.

	PAGE.
SUCCESSION OF PASTORS,	7
ORDER OF EXERCISES,	9
ACCOUNT OF THE CELEBRATION,	15
CORRESPONDENCE,	19
HISTORICAL DISCOURSE,	21

APPENDIX.

A.—Church organization, 1870, ... 151
B.—List of surnames of the earliest members of the congregation, ... 151
C.—Patent for church lands, ... 152
D.—Names of pewholders given on a draft of the old church, 153
E.—List of subscribers to rebuilding of graveyard wall in 1790, ... 154
F.—First call given to Rev. James Latta, . . . 155
G.—Charter of Incorporation, . . . 156
H.—List of Trustees, ... 158
J.—List of persons buried in the old "New Side" graveyard, 159
K.—List of persons buried in Upper Octorara graveyard, . 160
L.—Surnames of members of congregation, 1870, . 184

SUCCESSION OF PASTORS

OF

UPPER OCTORARA CHURCH.

REV. ADAM BOYD, ordained and installed October 13, 1724; resigned October 19, 1768; died November 23, 1768; pastor forty-four years.

REV. ANDREW STERLING, ordained and installed over the 2d or New Side Congregation, in 1747; deposed April 24, 1765; died in August, 1765; pastor eighteen years.

REV. WILLIAM FOSTER, ordained and installed over the United Congregation, October 19, 1768; died September 30, 1780; pastor nearly twelve years.
> From 1780 to 1785, the congregation was supplied by Presbytery.

REV. ALEXANDER MITCHEL, installed December 14, 1785; pastoral relation dissolved May 5, 1796; pastor nearly eleven years.
> From 1796 to 1810—fourteen years—the congregation was supplied by Presbytery.

REV. JAMES LATTA, took charge of the congregation October 1, 1810; ordained and installed April 2, 1811; pastoral relation dissolved October 1, 1850; pastor forty years.

REV. JAMES M. CROWELL, ordained and installed June 3, 1851; pastoral relation dissolved April 14, 1857; pastor nearly six years.

REV. ALEXANDER REED, ordained and installed October 8, 1857; pastoral relation dissolved October 20, 1864; pastor seven years.

REV. JOHN J. POMEROY—present pastor—installed November 14, 1865.

ORDER OF EXERCISES

AT THE

CELEBRATION OF THE 150TH ANNIVERSARY OF THE UPPER OCTORARA PRESBYTERIAN CHURCH,

SEPTEMBER 14, 1870.

FORENOON.

I. INVOCATION, by Rev. Thomas Love.
II. ANTHEM—"O Come Let us Sing."
III. READING OF SCRIPTURES, Psalm cxxii., by Rev. James L. Scott.
IV. PRAYER, by Rev. Justus T. Umsted.
V. HYMN.

> All people that on earth do dwell,
>   Sing to the Lord with cheerful voice,
> Him serve with mirth, His praise forth tell,
>   Come ye before Him and rejoice.
>
> Know that the Lord is God indeed,
>   Without our aid He did us make;
> We are His flock, He doth us feed,
>   And for His sheep, He doth us take.
>
> O enter then His gates with praise,
>   Approach with joy His courts unto:
> Praise, laud, and bless His name always,
>   For it is seemly so to do.

> Because the Lord our God is good,
>   His mercy is for ever sure;
> His truth at all times firmly stood,
>   And shall from age to age endure.

VI. HISTORICAL DISCOURSE, by J. Smith Futhey, Esq.

VII. SONG, "A Hundred Years to Come."

> Where! where will be the birds that sing,
>   A hundred years to come?
> The flowers that now in beauty spring,
>   A hundred years to come?
> The rosy lips, the lofty brow,
> The heart that beats so gaily now,
> O where will be love's beaming eye,
> Joy's pleasant smile, and sorrow's sigh
>   A hundred years to come?
>
> Who'll tread for gain these rural ways,
>   A hundred years to come?
> Who'll fill this church with songs of praise,
>   A hundred years to come?
> Pale, trembling age, and fiery youth,
> And childhood with its heart of truth,
> The rich, the poor, on land and sea,
> Where will the mighty millions be
>   A hundred years to come?
>
> We all within our graves shall sleep,
>   A hundred years to come?
> No living soul for us will weep,
>   A hundred years to come?
> But other men our lands will till,
> And others then our streets will fill,
> While other birds will sing as gay,
> And bright the sun shine as to-day,
>   A hundred years to come?

VIII. BENEDICTION, by Rev. B. B. Hotchkin.

ORDER OF EXERCISES.

AFTERNOON

I. ANTHEM.
II. PRAYER, by Rev. E. E. Adams. D.D.
III. HYMN.

    How did my heart rejoice to hear
      My friends devoutly say,
    "In Sion let us all appear,
      And keep the solemn day."

    I love her gates, I love the road;
      The church, adorned with grace,
    Stands like a palace built for God,
      To show His milder face.

    Peace be within this sacred place,
      And joy a constant guest;
    With holy gifts and heavenly grace
      Be her attendants blest.

    My soul shall pray for Sion still,
      While life or breath remains;
    There my best friends, my kindred dwell,
      There God, my Saviour, reigns.

IV. REMARKS ON PRESBYTERIANISM, by Rev. Nathan Grier Parke.

V. HYMN.

    I love Thy kingdom, Lord,
      The house of Thine abode,
    The church our blest Redeemer saved
      With his own precious blood.

    I love Thy church, O God!
      Her walls before Thee stand,
    Dear as the apple of Thine eye,
      And graven on Thy hand.

    For her my tears shall fall,
      For her my prayers ascend,
    To her my cares and toils be given,
      Till toils and cares shall end.

Beyond my highest joy
  I prize her heavenly ways,
Her sweet communion, solemn vows,
  Her hymns of love and praise.

Jesus, Thou Friend divine,
  Our Saviour and our King,
Thy hand from every snare and foe
  Shall great deliverance bring.

Sure as Thy truth shall last,
  To Sion shall be given
The brightest glories earth can yield,
  And brighter bliss of heaven.

VI. PERSONAL REMINISCENCES, by Rev. John L. Withrow and Rev. Samuel T. Lowrie.

VII. HYMN.

God bless our native land!
Firm may she ever stand
  Through storm and night;
When the wild tempests rave,
Ruler of winds and wave,
Do Thou our country save,
  By Thy great might.

For her our pray'rs shall rise
To God above the skies,—
  On Him we wait;
Thou who has heard each sigh,
Watching each weeping eye,
Be Thou for ever nigh;
  God save the State.

Our fathers' God! to Thee,
Author of liberty,
  To Thee we sing:
Long may our land be bright
With freedom's holy light;
Protect us by Thy might,
  Great God our King.

ORDER OF EXERCISES.

VIII. PASTORAL REMINISCENCES, by Rev. James M. Crowell, D.D., and Rev. Alexander Reed, D.D.

IX. DOXOLOGY.

>Glory be to God the Father,
>Glory be to th' eternal Son,
>Glory to the Holy Spirit.
>Hail the blessed Three in One;
>Hallelujah!
>Hail the blessed Three in One.

X. BENEDICTION, by Rev. M. B. Grier, D.D.

ACCOUNT OF THE CELEBRATION.

BY ALFRED P. REID, ESQ.

At a meeting of the Session of Upper Octorara Church, in 1869, the pastor—Rev. John J. Pomeroy—suggested the propriety of celebrating the one hundred and fiftieth anniversary of founding the church.

The suggestion was at once acted upon, and J. Smith Futhey, Esq., of West Chester, Pa., a son of the Church, and a gentleman noted for his love of antiquarian research, was invited to prepare the historical address for the occasion.

Wednesday, September 14th, 1870, was subsequently fixed upon as the day for the celebration.

It was a beautiful autumnal day; nature seemed in harmony with the occasion, and smiled benignantly upon this rural spot, among the old oaks, beside the silent resting place of an honored ancestry.

The trustees had recently repaired the church building, recushioned the pews, and put the graveyard in order at considerable toil and expense. Everything presented a neat and comfortable appearance, and one could cheerfully yield himself up to the associations of the past, and the enjoyments of the occasion.

Although but a limited notice had been given of the Anniversary, there was such a gathering as these sacred precincts had never witnessed. Crowds of people came from far and near, many of them had not seen the church for years, some never, but ties of affinity and attachment to this venerable pillar of the truth, drew them aside from their ordinary avocations to this celebration. The meeting house was crowded to overflowing, long before the hour for the exercises to begin, arrived.

Few churches in our country can trace back their history as far as Upper Octorara. It is one of the early landmarks of Presbyterianism in our land.

Within its fold have lived earnest, holy lives, spent in the service of the church. From it have gone out men rich in intellectual and moral worth, and of exalted aims. Many streams of blessings scattered far and wide, trace their source to this well-spring of Zion. Very proud of her history are those who have grown up under the shadow of old Octorara Church.

There came up to this festival many of the clergy, especially of the old Presbytery of New Castle, with which the church was so long connected. The following were present:—Rev. James M. Crowell, D.D., of St. Peters' Church, Rochester, N. Y.; Rev. Alexander Reed, D.D., of the Central Church, Philadelphia, both of whom were former pastors of the church; Rev. John J. Pomeroy, its present pastor; Rev. Thomas Love, one of the oldest living members of New Castle Presbytery; Rev. Alexander G. Morrison, of Coatesville; Rev. John M. Dickey, D.D., of Oxford; Rev. Philip J. Timlow, of Leacock Church, Lancaster County; Rev. Ezra E. Adams, D.D., Professor in Lincoln University; Rev. Beriah B. Hotchkin, of Marple Church, Delaware County; Rev. Justus T. Umsted, of Faggs' Manor Church; Rev. Matthew B. Grier, D.D., editor of the Presbyterian, Philadelphia; Rev. Nathan Grier Parke, of Pittston, Luzerne County; Rev. James L. Scott, Principal of Seminary, Hammonton, New Jersey; Rev. William F. P. Noble, of Penningtonville; Rev. Joseph M. Rittenhouse, of Middle Octorara; Rev. Lorenzo Westcott, Professor in Lincoln University; Rev. Joseph S. Gilmer, of Kennett Square; Rev. Samuel T. Lowrie, of Abington, Montgomery County; Rev. John L. Withrow, of Arch Street Church, Philadelphia; Rev. David W. Moore, of Lower Brandywine Church, Delaware; Rev. John P. Clarke, of Little Valley Church, Mifflin County; Rev. Anthony C. Junkin, of Red Clay Creek Church, Delaware; Rev. James Roberts, of Coatesville; Rev. John Rea, of Downingtown; Rev. William W. Heberton, of Brandywine Manor, and Rev. William W. Dalbey, Pastor of the Baptist Church in Penningtonville.

ACCOUNT OF THE CELEBRATION. 17

The exercises, which were well arranged and admirably suited to the occasion, were presided over by the Rev. John J. Pomeroy. The Historical Address occupied two hours in its delivery, and was listened to with the utmost attention, and unflagging interest, by the vast congregation. The Historian had not time to present all the material he had gathered together. His intimate acquaintance with the antiquarian history of the county, and especially of this part of it, the place of his birth, had enabled him to draw upon stores accessible to few but himself. It was an exceedingly valuable discourse, chaste in its diction, admirably blending the details of history with the quaint usages and reminiscences of the past, and enlivening the dry bones of minute facts with the anecdotes and humor of the times as preserved in tradition.

At its conclusion, the audience was dismissed to partake of the bountiful refreshments the people of the congregation had provided. The arrangements for this object were admirable, and the temporal wants of all were abundantly supplied.

After an hour thus spent, and in social intercourse, and in visiting the adjacent cemetery, the congregation reassembled.

Rev. N. G. Parke was introduced and spoke on Presbyterianism; lucidly sketching its history and characteristics.

Rev. John L. Withrow, son of a former ruling elder in Upper Octorara, touchingly referred to his early associations in the church, and to personal incidents connected therewith.

Rev. Samuel T. Lowrie, a descendant of the first elder Arthur Parke, also gave some personal reminiscences of his family, and their connection with this church.

J. Smith Futhey, Esq., read interesting letters from several of the descendants of the Rev. William Foster, a pastor of the church in the olden time.

Dr. Crowell and Dr. Reed spoke of their connection with the church, and paid fitting tributes to the many good men and women, now deceased, with whom they were associated while pastors, and to the affection and esteem which they had ever had from the congregation, and gave interesting reminiscences of their pastorates.

The music was excellent,—good, old fashioned congregational singing, such as we love,—led by a well trained choir.

The shades of evening were drawing close around before the vast assembly broke up and dispersed to their homes. It was a day long to be remembered in the annals of the church—a day when old associations were renewed, ties of Christian friendship strengthened, and the broken links in her history re-united. It will long live in our memory as a day replete with profitable thought and reflection, and delightful entertainment.

CORRESPONDENCE.

UPPER OCTORARA MANSE,
September 24, 1870.

J. SMITH FUTHEY, ESQ.,

DEAR SIR: Your admirable Historical Address, delivered on the occasion of the one hundred and fiftieth Anniversary of the Upper Octorara Presbyterian Church, has created the very general desire on the part of our congregation and friends of our Church, to see it in printed form.

At a joint meeting of the Session and Board of Trustees, the undersigned were appointed a committee to make known to you this desire, and to respectfully solicit a copy of your Address for publication. We earnestly hope this urgent request will meet with your favorable response.

Very truly and sincerely, Yours,

JOHN J. POMEROY,
Pastor of Upper Octorara Church.

SAMUEL WALKER,
Ruling Elder.

GEORGE M. BOYD,
President of Board of Trustees.

WEST CHESTER, PA., *Oct.* 3, 1870.

GENTLEMEN: In compliance with your request, I herewith place at your disposal the discourse delivered on the occasion of the one hundred and fiftieth Anniversary of the Upper Octorara Presbyterian Church.

The task of its preparation—undertaken at the request of the Session of the Church—was to me a very grateful one, and the consciousness that it has been esteemed of sufficient value to justify its committal to the press, is an abundant reward for the labor bestowed upon it.

Thanking you for the kindness of the terms in which the request has been conveyed,

     I remain, Gentlemen,
      Your obedient servant,
       J. SMITH FUTHEY.

To
 REV. JOHN J. POMEROY,
 MR. SAMUEL WALKER,   *Committee.*
 MR. GEORGE M. BOYD,

HISTORICAL DISCOURSE.

Remember the days of old, consider the years of many generations; ask thy father and he will show thee; thy elders, and they will tell thee.—Deuteronomy xxxii. 7.

Walk about Zion, and go round about her; tell the towers thereof. Mark ye well her bulwarks, consider her palaces: that ye may tell it to the generation following.—Psalm xlviii. 12, 13.

It is a time honored usage of all civilized people, to commemorate leading events of their past history. The Jews had their periods for thanksgiving and rejoicing, in commemoration of great national events, such as the feast of the Passover and the Jubilean festivals; and their days of fasting, commemorative of particular national calamities, such as the fall of Jerusalem. A portion of the Christian world hold in especial reverence the supposed birth-day of the Saviour of mankind, and of that in which he rose from the dead, and in the memorial feast of the Lord's Supper, we commemorate an event, the most astounding that has ever transpired in this fallen world. There is scarcely a nation or people, who have not *some* memorial usages by which to renew the recollection of great events. We, as Americans, observe as holidays the anniversary of the natal day of him who is not inappropriately styled "the Father of his country," and of the day in which, as a nation, we flung our banner to the breeze and bade defiance to the power that would enslave us.

And we have come here to-day, to celebrate what may be appropriately termed, the sesqui-centennial anniversary of the existence of this Church.

A century and a half has been accomplished, since a congregation of Presbyterian emigrants met on this spot, to worship the only living and true God, in the simple forms used by them in the land of their birth; and from that day to this, on almost every returning Sabbath, a congregation of worshipers has met here, the everlasting truth has been proclaimed, and the sound of prayer and praise has ascended to the most High.

There are interesting associations connected with the history of this Church and its surroundings. It takes us back to a period when the country here was new, and very thinly settled—when it was the home and the hunting ground of the Indian. It takes us back to the colonial days of our country—to a period less than one hundred years from the landing of the Pilgrims on Plymouth Rock, and but thirty-eight years after the arrival of William Penn. Aside from Philadelphia and a few very small neighboring towns, such as Chester and New Castle, the country here and in parts adjacent, was then—with few exceptions—almost an unbroken wilderness.

It is true, one hundred and fifty years is not a very long time in the history of an old nation, but in ours, it is. To those accustomed to look upon the hoary castles of the old world—those monuments of a thousand years—that date to the time of the Crusades and beyond, a century and a half may seem but a brief space of time; but to us, whose past extends but a little way back, ere it is lost in dimness and uncertainty, "a hundred and fifty years ago," seems to belong to a remote age.

When we reflect that it is but a little over three hundred and fifty years since the existence of this Continent was made known to the European powers; that it is little more than half that period since the spot where Philadelphia now stands was a forest, occupied by the Red Man, we see that this Church is one of no inconsiderable American antiquity.

The Session of this Church have esteemed the present period, a suitable one in which to take a retrospective glance at her past history, and to trace it from its obscure beginnings, through its different phases, down to the present time, and they have invited me to the performance of this grateful, but somewhat laborious task.

In the performance of this duty, I have endeavored to carry out the spirit of the words of Moses which I have just quoted. I have—so far as the sources were available—remembered for you the days of old in the history of the Church, and considered the years of the generations which have elapsed since its foundations were laid. I have asked the fathers, and they have showed me; I have consulted the elders, and they have told me, and the information which I have thus gathered, meagre though it may be, I come—as far as I am able—to set in order before you to-day.

In this review, it is natural that we should attach a particular feeling of interest to the olden time ; for societies as well as individuals, are not without curiosity at least, and perhaps pride, in relation to their ancestry. And the Christian will ever turn to the church of his choice, as an institution claiming his affectionate regard, and its history, even back to the feeble beginning, should possess for him the highest interest.

In endeavoring however to trace the *early* history of this Church, I have been met with a difficulty similar to that experienced by the children of Israel, when they were required by their task-masters to make bricks without straw; but unlike the children of Israel, who were compelled to gather straw for themselves, I have been kindly and cheerfully furnished with such materials as were accessible.

No records are to be found of the doings of the Session, during the first ninety years of her existence. It is highly probable that none were kept. This neglect, which seems to have been common with the Presbyterian churches of this country, has been the subject of regret with almost every one who has been engaged in investigating their early history. Our early pastors and sessions seem not to have heeded the exhortation of the Psalmist, " to walk about Zion and go round about her, and tell the towers thereof; to mark well her bulwarks and consider her palaces, that they might tell it to the generation following." Had they done so, the labors of the historian would have been greatly lightened, and his narrative been correspondingly more interesting. And this neglect does not seem to have arisen, from the want of their attention being called to it, for I find on the early records of the Presbytery of New Castle, under date of September 12. 1717, this entry: "Appointed, that the respective ministers, members of this Presbytery, do endeavor to keep a session-book in their respective congregations."

"I regard it as the solemn duty of every church, to keep a faithful record of its history, and thus afford the opportunity to succeeding generations to know something of its origin, its progress, its vicissitudes, its foes, its struggles and its triumphs."

The ancient Jews were required "to instruct their children, that they might convey throughout all generations, the history of those divine interpositions and mercies with which they had been favored," and the obligation is no less binding upon Christian churches, thus to keep in perpetual remembrance, the dealings of God with them, for the information and encouragement of succeeding generations. I am happy to say, that the later records of this church, both the sessional records, and those kept by the trustees, are remarkably complete and accurate, and that its history, during the present generation, may be found very fully embodied in them.

The province of Pennsylvania was early attractive to emigrants from other countries. It was recommended by its free government, by the character of its fundamental laws, its fertile soil, salubrious and temperate climate, its adaptation to a rural population, with advantages for trade, commerce and manufactures.

These emigrants were from various parts of Europe. They were not homogeneous, but were diversified by their origin, religious principles, habits and language. This diversity, arising from their different nationalities, divided them into three distinctly marked classes, whose separation was maintained unbroken for many generations, and is not yet effaced.

It is a singular fact that the white races in Pennsylvania are remarkably unmixed, and retain their original character beyond that of any state in the Union. These distinctly marked races are the English, the German and the Scotch and Scotch-Irish. Emigrants from other countries contributed to swell the population. Among the choicest of the early settlers were the Swedes, the Welsh, the Huguenots, the Hollanders and the Swiss; but their numbers were small compared with those of the races I have just mentioned, and their peculiar characteristics, through admixture with the people of other nationalities, and the mellowing influence of time, are scarcely recognizable.

The associates and followers of Penn, known as Friends or Quakers, who were mainly of English descent, were amongst the first emigrants, and settled chiefly in Philadelphia and the country near it, embracing what is now Delaware County, the eastern and central portions of Chester County, and the southern parts of Bucks and Montgomery counties. They were an orderly, industrious and law abiding people, cultivating peace with all men.

The Germans, who came in large numbers, were of different denominations of Christians, principally Lutheran and German Reformed, with some Mennonites, Dunkers, Moravians, Amish and others. They were orderly, industrious and frugal farmers, peaceful and honest in their relations and dealings; a people that emphatically minded their own business, and made continual accessions to their wealth.

The third race—with which we are more immediately concerned—were the Scotch and Scotch-Irish, who constituted a considerable portion of the early settlers of Pennsylvania, and from whom the greater portion of the audience before me are descended. It may not be inappropriate before proceeding further, to refer briefly to the history of this race previous to their emigration to our shores, and I do this the more readily, inasmuch as I have found in my intercourse with the people, that beyond the fact that they came principally from the north of Ireland, little seems to be known of them; and this ignorance is common, even among their descendants.

During the Irish rebellions in the reign of Elizabeth, the province of Ulster, embracing the northern counties of Ireland, was reduced to the lowest extremity of poverty and wretchedness; and its moral and religious state was scarcely less deplorable than its civil. Soon after the accession of James I., his quarrels with the Roman Catholics of that Province, led to a conspiracy against the British authority. O'Neill and O'Donnell, two Irish lords, who had been created earls by the English government—the former the Earl of Tyrone, and the latter the Earl of Tyrconnel—arranged a plot against the government. Its detection led these chief conspirators to fly the country, leaving their extensive estates—about 500,000 acres—at the mercy of the king, who only wanted a pretext for taking possession. A second insurrection soon gave occasion for another large forfeiture, and nearly six entire counties in the province of Ulster were confiscated and subjected to the disposal of the crown. But it was a territory which showed the effects of a long series of lawless disturbances. It was almost depopulated, its resources wasted, and the cultivation of the soil in a great measure abandoned. The state of society—such as existed—was in keeping with the physical aspect of the country.

It became a favorite project with the king, to repeople those counties with a Protestant population, who would be disposed to the arts of peace and industry; the better to preserve order, to establish more firmly the British rule, and to introduce a higher state of cultivation into that portion of his domains. To promote this object, liberal offers of land were made, and other inducements held out in England and Scotland for colonists to occupy this wide and vacant territory. This was about the year 1610. The project was eagerly embraced, companies and colonies were formed, and individuals without organization were tempted to partake of the advantageous offers of the government. A London company—among the first to enter upon this new acquisition—established itself at Derry, and gave such character to the place, as to cause it to be known and called the city of London-Derry.

The principal emigration however, was from Scotland. Its coast is within twenty miles of the County of Antrim in Ireland, and across this strait flowed from the north-east, a large population distinguished for thrift, industry and endurance; and bringing with them their Presbyterianism and rigid adherence to the Westminster standards. They settled principally in the counties of Down, Londonderry and Antrim; and have given a peculiar and elevated character to that portion of the Emerald Isle.

This was the first Protestant population that was introduced into Ireland; and the Presbyterians of Scotland, who thus furnished the largest element, have maintained their ascendency to the present day, against the persevering efforts of the government church on the one hand, and the Romanists, by whom they were surrounded, on the other. The first Presbyterian church established in Ireland, was in the county of Antrim, in 1613.

The province, in consequence of this influx of population, greatly revived and continued for some years to advance in prosperity. The towns were replenished with inhabitants, the lands were cleared, and houses erected throughout the country.

But it was a day in which the throne of Britain

was governed by bigotry and despotism. Persecutions of an oppressive nature began in Ulster in 1661, and every expedient—short of utter extirpation—was tried, to break down the attachment of the people to their Presbyterian polity; but, as is always the case, these persecutions only attached the people the stronger to their faith. Many ministers were deposed and forced to return to Scotland.

The tide however presently changed. Persecutions ceased in Ireland and the scene was transferred to Scotland. The latter Stuarts—Charles II. and James II.—blind to the dictates of justice and humanity, pursued a system of measures best calculated to wean from their support their Presbyterian subjects, who were bound to them by national prejudice and had been most devoted to their kingly cause, and to whose assistance Charles II. owed his restoration to the throne. Sir James Grahame, better known as Claverhouse, was sent to Scotland with his dragoons, upon the mistaken mission of compelling the Presbyterians to conform in their religious worship to that of the establishment; and from 1670, until the accession of William and Mary, the Presbyterians of Scotland worshiped in hidden places, and at the peril of their lives.

The attempts to establish "the Church of England" over Scotland, and destroy the religious system so universally established and so dearly cherished by that devoted people, was pursued by the Charleses and James II., by persecutions as mean, cruel, and savage as any which have disgraced the annals of religious bigotry and crime. Many were treacherously and ruthlessly butchered, and the ministers were prohibited under severe penalties from preaching, baptizing or ministering in any way to their flocks.

Worn out with the unequal contest, these persistent and enduring Presbyterians, having suffered to the extreme of cruelty and oppression, abandoned the land of their birth and sought an asylum among their countrymen who had preceded them in the secure retreats of Ulster; and thither they escaped as best they could, some crossing the narrow sea in open boats. They carried their household gods with them, and their religious peculiarities became more dear in their land of exile, for the dangers and sorrows through which they had borne them.

This is the race—composed of various tribes, flowing from different parts of Scotland—which furnished the population in the north of Ireland, familiarly known as the Scotch-Irish. This term Scotch-Irish, does not denote an admixture of the Scotch and Irish races. The one did not intermarry with the other. The Scotch were principally Saxon in blood and Presbyterian in religion; the native Irish Celtic in blood and Roman Catholic in religion; and these were elements which could not very readily coalesce. Hence the races are as distinct in Ireland at the present day, after the lapse of two centuries and a half, as when the Scotch first took up their abode in that island. They were called Scotch-Irish, simply from the circumstance that they were the descendants of Scots, who had taken up their residence in the north of Ireland.

I may observe, that the term "Scotch-Irish,"—although expressive—is purely American. In Ireland it is not used. There, in contra-distinction to the native or Celtic Irish, they are called Scotch.

These people, by their industry, frugality and skill, made the region into which they thus moved, comparatively a rich and flourishing country. They improved agriculture, and introduced manufactures, and by the excellence and high reputation of their productions, attracted trade and commerce to their markets.

The government however, soon began to recognize them, in the shape of taxes and embarrassing regulations upon their industry and trade. These restrictions, together with an extravagant advance in rents by landlords whose long leases had now expired, occasioned much distress, and the people were brought to a state of degrading subjection to England, and many of them reduced to comparative poverty.

Their patience was at length exhausted, and these energetic and self-willed Scotch-Irish, animated by the same spirit which subsequently moved the American mind in the days of the Revolution, determined no longer to endure these oppressive measures, and they sought by another change of residence to find a freer field for the exercise of their industry and skill, and for the enjoyment of their religion.

Ireland was not the home of their ancestors; it was endeared to them by no traditions, and numbers of them determined to quit it, and seek in the American wilds a better home than they had in the old world.

Accordingly, about the beginning of the eighteenth century, they commenced to emigrate to the American colonies in large numbers. The spirit of emigration—fostered no doubt by the glowing accounts sent home by their countrymen who had preceded them—seized these people to such an extent, that it threatened almost a total depopulation. Such multitudes of husbandmen, laborers and manufacturers flocked over the Atlantic, that the landlords began to be alarmed, and to concert ways and means for preventing the growing evil. Scarce a ship sailed for the colonies, that was not crowded with men, women and children. They came for a time principally to Pennsylvania; although some of them settled in New England, and others found their way to the Carolinas. It is stated by Proud, in his history of Pennsylvania, that by the year 1729, six thousand Scotch-Irish had come to that colony, and that before the middle of the century, nearly twelve thousand arrived annually for several years. In September 1736, alone, one thousand families sailed from Belfast, on account of the difficulty of renewing their leases.

They were Protestants, and generally Presbyterians—few or none of the Catholic Irish came until after the Revolution. The settlement of this latter class in this country, is comparatively of modern date.

Extensive emigrations from the northern counties of Ireland, were principally made at two distinct periods of time. The first,—of which I have been speaking—from about the year 1718 to the middle of the century; the second, from about 1771 to 1773, although "there was a gentle current westward between these two eras."

The cause of this second extensive emigration was somewhat similar to that of the first. It is well known that a greater portion of the lands in Ireland, are owned by a comparatively small number of proprietors, who rent them to the farming classes on long leases. In 1771, the leases on an estate in the county of Antrim—the property of the Marquis of Donegal—having expired, the rents were so largely advanced, that many of the tenants could not comply with the demands, and were deprived of the farms they had occupied. This aroused a spirit of resentment to the oppression of the large landed proprietors, and an immediate and extensive emigration to America was the consequence. From 1771 to 1773, there sailed from the ports in the north of Ireland, nearly one hundred vessels, carrying as many as twenty-five thousand passengers, all Presbyterians. This was shortly before the breaking out of the Revolutionary war, and these people, leaving the old world in such a temper, became a powerful contribution to the cause of liberty, and to the separation of the colonies from the mother country.

These Scotch-Irish emigrants landed principally at New Castle and Philadelphia, and found their way northward and westward into the eastern and middle counties of Pennsylvania. From thence, one stream followed the great Cumberland Valley into Virginia and North Carolina, and from these, colonies passed into Kentucky and Tennessee. Another powerful body went into western Pennsylvania, and settling on the head waters of the Ohio, became famous both in civil and ecclesiastical history, and have given to the region around Pittsburgh, the name it so well deserves, of being the back-bone of Presbyterianism.

The first settlement in *this* region of country, was made by the Scotch-Irish about the year 1718. They gradually spread over the whole western portion of Chester County, from Maryland and Delaware on the south, to the chain of hills known as the Welsh mountain on the north; and the greater portion of the population of this district of country at the present day, are their descendants. These early emigrants planted the Presbyterian churches at Upper Octorara, Faggs Manor, Brandywine Manor, New London and Oxford, in this county; and these churches abide in strength to the present day.

It is said to be a hard thing to kill a Presbyterian Church, and this is exemplified not only in those planted in this county, but throughout the country. Of course, this is only true as a general rule. Presbyterian churches may—from emigration and other causes—become weakened and eventually cease to exist, but it will be found on examination, that they are more tenacious of life than those of any other denomination.

Such is a brief sketch of the early history of the people known as the Scotch-Irish, and of their emigration and settlement in this country.

This race, "in energy, enterprise, intelligence, education, patriotism. religious and moral character, the maintenance of civil and religious liberty, and inflexable resistance to all usurpation in church and state, were not surpassed by any class of settlers in the American colonies."

In the struggle for popular rights, they were ever found on the side of the people, and the maintenance of freedom in religious worship, was with them a cardinal principle.

Pennsylvania owes much of what she is to-day, to the fact that so many of these people settled within her borders. Probably not less than five millions of people in America, have the blood of these Scotch and Scotch-Irish in their veins, and there is not one of them, man or woman. that is not proud of it, or that would exchange it for any other lineage.

"The first public voice in America for dissolving all connection with Great Britain," says Bancroft, "came from the Scotch-Irish Presbyterians." A large number of them were signers of the Declaration of Independence, and throughout the revolution they were devoted to the cause of the country. Such a thing as a Scotch-Irish tory was unheard of; the race never produced one. It was the energy and devotion of this people that sustained the army in the field in the many dark hours of that contest, and which under the guidance of Providence, carried this country successfully through the struggle for freedom.

When the subject of the dissolution of all connection between the colonies and the mother country was before the Continental Congress, it was John

Witherspoon, a Scotch Presbyterian clergyman, and a descendant of John Knox, who is reported to have said, "That noble instrument on your table, which secures immortality to its author, should be subscribed this very morning by every pen in this house. He who will not respond to its accents, and strain every nerve to carry into effect its provisions, is unworthy the name of a freeman. Although these gray hairs must descend into the sepulchre, I would infinitely rather they would descend thither by the hand of the public executioner, than desert, at this crisis, the sacred cause of my country!"—words which were potent in securing the adoption of the Declaration of Independence.

Many of the most eminent men in the nation are, and have been of this race. It has furnished five Presidents of the United States, seven Governors of Pennsylvania, a majority of the judges of this state, and a full proportion of the legislators, state and national, and of those who have occupied other high official positions.

In the church, we may well be proud of the names of those who have ministered at her altars. A race, which has produced such men as John Witherspoon, the Tennants, father and sons, Samuel and John Blair, Francis Alison, the Duffields, the Alexanders, Robert Smith and his sons, Samuel Stanhope Smith and John Blair Smith, has proven that it is not of ignoble blood, and that it is second to none on the face of the earth with which it may be compared.

The race is noted for its firmness, perseverance and

undaunted energy in whatever it undertakes, and those characteristics have aided in carrying it successively through many a conflict. Whatever an individual with Scotch blood predominating in his veins undertakes, he generally performs, if in his power.

When John Knox was laid in his grave, the Earl of Morton—then recently appointed regent—who stood by, is said to have pronounced his eulogium in these, or similar words: "There lies he, who never feared the face of man." And what was true of John Knox, may be said of the race, "It never shrinks from responsibilities, and it fears not the face of man."

Its character for firmness—perhaps it might be called stubbornness—is somewhat facetiously, but well illustrated in the prayer of the Scotch elder, who besought the Lord that he might be always right, adding, "for thou knowest Lord, that I am very hard to turn," or, as expressed in the Scottish dialect, "ye ken Lord, that I am unco hard to turn."

We will now turn from this cursory glance at the history of the race to which most of us belong, and direct our attention to that of this Church. which as already observed, was founded by emigrants from the province of Ulster, and which has been mainly maintained by their descendants.

The township of Sadsbury, in which this church is situated, was organized at a very early day. Originally, it extended indefinitely westward, but by the erection of Lancaster county in 1729, the Octorara creek became its western boundary, and that portion of the township west of the creek, became known as

Sadsbury township, in Lancaster county. The name is English. It was originally settled by both Quakers and Presbyterians, and the population ever since, has been of a mixed character.

This congregation was formed—as near as can now be ascertained—in the year 1720. As there is no record of its organization, we can only approximate the time when the people first assembled on this spot for religious worship. This is believed to have been in the fall of the year 1720—one hundred and fifty years ago.

It was originally known as *Sadsbury*. The first minister who preached here was the Rev. David Evans. Mr. Evans had been pastor of the congregation of the Welsh tract, in New Castle county, Delaware, but difficulties arising between him and some of his people, the pastoral relation was dissolved. This was in May, 1720. He then, as appears from the minutes of Presbytery, supplied the people of Tredyffrin, now known as the Great Valley church, and was also sent by the Presbytery to the region now called Octorara, Forks of Brandywine and Conestoga, extending to Donegal and even beyond. The whole territory thus included, was missionary ground, and Mr. Evans preached in various places in the different settlements which had been formed. In June, 1721, he was directed by the Presbytery to supply the same people, and a letter was directed to be written by Mr. Cross, to the people at Tredyffrin, and "the people at Sadsbury, upon the western branches of Brandywine," and the people at Conestoga. In August, 1721, Mr. Evans reported to Presbytery that he had supplied the people of Tredyffrin, and Sadsbury, and Conestoga. Mr. Cross also reported, that he had written to the people of Sadsbury according to appointment. Mr. Evans was again appointed to supply the people at Tredyffrin, and directed "to allow every fourth Sabbath day to the people at Sadsbury." In September, 1721, the name of *Octorara* first appears upon the minutes of Presbytery. It is recorded that "a letter from the people of Sadsbury (alias Akterara), to this Presbytery being read, was referred to the committee on bills and overtures."

This is the last time that *Sadsbury* is mentioned as the name of this congregation; thereafter it is called Octorara. The first syllable of the name Octorara, would seem originally to have been pronounced *Ac*, as in the early minutes of Presbytery it is spelled Akterara, Ackterara, Acterara, Actarara. We indeed, sometimes hear it so pronounced at the present day.

The name "Upper Octorara," was first given to this church about the year 1727, to distinguish it from Middle Octorara, in Lancaster County; and from the church now called Lower West Nottingham, in Maryland, which was originally known as "Mouth of Octorara," and subsequently as "Lower Octorara."

Mr. Evans continued to supply this congregation until March, 1723, when Rev. Daniel Macgill was appointed to have the oversight of it. He supplied it until his death on February 10, 1724. In April, 1724, Rev. David Evans was again directed by Presbytery, to "supply ye people of Actarara with preaching every fourth Sabbath." He did so until July 1724, when he ceased to act in that capacity.

The congregation was directed by the Presbytery "to gratify the ministers sent to them, and not let them go home unpaid." They would seem from this injunction, to have been a little remiss in the performance of the duty they owed to those who were sent to break unto them the bread of life.

Mr. Evans, who was thus the first minister to this congregation, was a native of Wales, from whence he emigrated about the year 1701, graduated at Yale College in 1713, was ordained in 1714, and besides thus supplying Octorara for a time, was pastor of the Great Valley Church in Tredyffrin township for about twenty years. He afterwards accepted a call to a church in New Jersey, where he labored until his death, about the year 1750. He was recording clerk of the Presbytery of New Castle from its organization, March 13, 1716–7, until September 23, 1721, and his penmanship, as exhibited in the records of Presbytery, was in the extreme curious. His education and attainments were of a high grade. In 1748, he published a work, entitled "Law and Gospel; or, Man wholly Ruined by the Fall, and Recovered by the Gospel," being the substance of several sermons preached in 1734, at Tredyffrin from Gal. iii. 10, and Rom. i. 16. He was an eccentric and high spirited man, excitable and somewhat vascillating in his course.

Mr. Macgill, who, as already stated, ministered to

this congregation for about one year, was a native of Scotland, and came to this country about 1712, in September of which year he was received as a member of Presbytery. He is said to have been somewhat austere in his manners, but a good preacher and a learned man. The following advertisement, which is nearly all that has been rescued concerning him from the river of oblivion, is deemed worthy of preservation as an item of the olden time: "1722, Ran away from the Rev. D. Magill, a servant clothed with damask breeches, black broad-cloth vest, broad-cloth coat of copper colour and trimmed with black, and wearing black stockings." In reading this advertisement describing the dress of the servant, we may well exclaim, "If the servant was not greater than his master, what must the master have been?"

The Rev. Adam Boyd, who was the first regular pastor of this Church, was born in Ballymena, county Antrim, Ireland, in 1692, and came to New England as a probationer in 1722 or 1723. While there, he preached at Dedham. After remaining there for a time, he concluded to return to his native country, and was furnished by the celebrated Cotton Mather —who esteemed him well—with a certificate of his good character in this country, dated June 10, 1724. He, however, had formed an attachment to a daughter of Rev. Thomas Craighead, one of the pioneers of the Irish Presbyterians of New England, and, relinquishing his design of returning home, came to Pennsylvania, whither Mr. Craighead and his family had shortly preceded him, bringing with him the commendatory letter of Cotton Mather, as well as credentials from Ireland, and was received under the care of New Castle Presbytery. The following is the minute of Presbytery on the occasion of his reception: "July 29, 1724. The testimonials of Mr. Adam Boyd, preacher of the gospel, lately come from New England, were read and approved, and he being interrogated by the moderator, whether he would submit to this Presbytery, he answered that he would, during his abode in these parts." Mr. Craighead had been received as a member of Presbytery on January 28, 1723–4.

A copy, in Cotton Mather's hand-writing, of the letter given by him to Mr. Boyd, has been preserved among the Mather MSS, in the library of the American Antiquarian Society, at Worcester, Massachusetts. It reads thus:

"BOSTON, N. E., *June* 10, 1724.

"Our worthy friend, Mr. Adam Boyd, being on a return to Europe, it is hereby certified, on his behalf, that for the years of his late sojourning in these parts of the world, his behaviour, so far as we understand, has been inoffensive and commendable, and such as hath justified the testimonials with which he arrived hither. And we make no doubt that he will make a report of the kind reception which he and others of his and our brethren coming from Scotland and Ireland hither, (whereof more than two or three are at this time acceptably exercising their ministry in our churches,) have found in this country, that will be very contrary to the misrepresentations which some disturbers of the peace have given of it.

"We implore the blessing of our gracious Lord upon his person and his voyage, and hope that wherever he may be disposed of, he may have the rewards and comforts of a patient continuance in well doing to attend him."

On the same day on which Mr. Boyd became a member of Presbytery, he was sent as a supply to Octorara, with directions to collect a congregation also at Pequea, and take the necessary steps towards its organization. He was so acceptable to the people that at the next meeting of Presbytery, September 14, 1724, a call was presented for his services as a pastor by Cornelius Rowan and Arthur Park, representatives of the people at Octorara and Pickqua. This call was accepted by him on the 6th of October, and at the urgent request of the commissioners who presented it, that an early day should be fixed for his ordination, the Presbytery met at the "Ackterara Meeting House" on the 13th of October, 1724, for that purpose.

At this meeting of Presbytery—the first held on this spot—there were present as members, Thomas Craighead, of White Clay creek, George Gillespie, of Head of Christiana, Henry Hook, of Drawyers, Thomas Evans, of Pencader, and Alexander Hutchinson, of Bohemia, ministers, and Peter Bouchelle, elder. Mr. Craighead presided as Moderator.

Mr. Boyd having passed the usual examination, the minutes of Presbytery record that "Proclamation being made three times by Mr. George Gillespie, at the door of the meeting-house of Octorara, that if any person had any thing to object against the ordaining of Mr. Adam Boyd, they should make it known to the Presbytery now sitting, and no objection being made, they proceeded to his ordination, solemnly setting him apart to the work of the ministry, with prayer and imposition of the hands of the Presbytery, Mr. Henry Hook preaching the ordination sermon, and presiding in the work."

Cornelius Rowan and Arthur Park, who represented the congregation in prosecuting the call for Mr. Boyd, were natives of the north of Ireland, and were, of course, among the very earliest settlers of this region. As they are the first names of which we have any mention in connection with this congregation, a brief reference to them may not be uninteresting.

Cornelius Rowan resided south of the present village of Cochranville, and was evidently somewhat advanced in years. He died in August, 1725, less than one year after the installation of Mr. Boyd. In his will he speaks of himself as "late from Ireland," and mentions his wife Ann "now in Ireland." He left a son Abraham Rowan, and a daughter Ann, the wife of James Cochran, of Octorara. The persons appointed to execute his will, were his son-in-law, James Cochran, James Moore of New London, and Rev. Adam Boyd, whom he calls "minister of Octorara." His daughter Ann, the wife of James Cochran, left seven children, Robert, John, George, Stephen, Jane, and James Cochran, and Ann, the wife of Rev. John Roan.

The Cochran family were among the early emigrants. Three brothers, David, Robert, and James came from Scotland, and settled in the neighborhood of the present village of Cochranville. Their descendants have been numerous, and some of them have occupied positions of honor and influence. Samuel Cochran, a descendant of James and his wife Ann, the daughter of Cornelius Rowan, and a son of Stephen Cochran, was for a number of years Surveyor General of Pennsylvania, and filled the office of State Senator. The Cochrans were among the early members of this congregation. Some time after the organization of Fagg's Manor, they transferred their membership to that church, it being nearer their place of abode. James Cochran was one of its first ruling elders. Their place of burial, however, has always, until recently, been in the graveyard of this Church, where numerous stones, erected to perpetuate the memory of the different members of the family, may be seen.

Arthur Park was a native of Ballylagby, in county Donegal, Ireland. He, with his wife Mary and four children, Joseph, John and Samuel Park, and a daughter, the wife of William Noblett, came to this country prior to 1724. His brothers, Samuel and David, and his sister Jane, emigrated at the same time.

Arthur Park took up by warrant all the lands now embraced in the farms occupied by Adam Reid, Hood Reece, John Parke, John Andrew Parke, J. Wilson Hershberger, Walter Sutton and brother, and S. Butler Windle. He resided in the house formerly occupied by J. Wilson Hershberger, a short distance west of the Limestone road, which was the homestead, and died there in February, 1740. He devised the lands I have mentioned to his sons Joseph and John, subject to the payment of legacies to the other heirs. These sons divided the real estate between them; Joseph taking the southern part, embracing the farms now of J. W. Hershberger, the Messrs. Sutton and S. B. Windle, and John taking the northern part, covering the farms now of John Park, Adam Reid, and Hood Reece. Joseph Park, after his father's death, resided for a time at the old homestead, and then sold his lands and removed to Georgia. John Park erected a dwelling on the part taken by him, where the present John Parke resides. He died July 28, 1787, at the age of eighty-one years. His wife Elizabeth died May 21, 1794, at the age of eighty-two years. Their children were Arthur, Joseph, John, William, Mary, Elizabeth, Jane, David and Samuel, the last of whom died young. The entire Parke family, in this section of the country, together with many families bearing other honored surnames, are their descendants. It has furnished this church with five ruling elders, in five successive generations,—two of them bearing the name of Arthur, and three that of John,—and has also furnished four ministers—the late Rev. Samuel Parke, and his son, Rev. Nathan Grier Parke, the Rev. Samuel T. Lowrie, and the Rev. John L. Withrow. The name was originally spelled *Park*, but the later generations spell it *Parke*. Members of the family of the seventh generation from the original Arthur Park, are present within these walls to-day.

When the emigrant Arthur Park came from Ireland, he brought with him, among other household articles, a pewter platter, about seventeen inches in diameter, which has been preserved, and is now in the possession of one of his descendants. The letters A. M. P., the initials of the names of Arthur and Mary Park, are stamped upon it.

The Rev. Adam Boyd, at the time of his ordination, was about thirty-two years of age. Ten days thereafter he was married to Jane, the daughter of Rev. Thomas Craighead. His field of labor, when he became the pastor of this church, was quite extensive, and embraced not only its present territory, but covered also that belonging to the present congregations of Fork of Brandywine, Middle Octorara, Leacock, Pequea, Donegal, Doe Run, Coatesville, Belleview, Waynesburg, Penningtonville, and the northern portion of Fagg's Manor. Donegal he gave up, in 1727. In the same year, the portion of the congregation residing on the west side of the Octorara creek, having considerably increased in numbers, received permission from Presbytery to erect a meeting-house and to organize a new congregation. The church known as Middle Octorara was accordingly organized, and received supplies from Presbytery until a regular pastor was installed. Mr. Boyd continued to preach to them until the year 1730.

In 1731, the people at Pequea, to whom Mr. Boyd had ministered a portion of his time from his first taking charge of this church, obtained his services regularly every sixth Sabbath, and he continued to minister to them until October, 1733, when his father-in-law, Rev. Thomas Craighead, received and accepted a call from them, and was installed as their regular pastor.

Mr. Boyd, on the first of January, 1727, purchased from William Pusey two hundred and fifty acres of land in Sadsbury township, embracing the present farm of the late Rev. James Latta, and the late William Armstrong, and erected thereon a stone dwelling house, wherein he resided during the remainder of his life, and where he reared a large family. The dwelling house thus erected forms the front part of the present residence of Mrs. Latta. A few years thereafter, he took out a warrant and obtained a patent for about two hundred acres adjoining, comprising the present farms of Joseph C. Boyd, and that known as the Black Horse farm, of the late John Boyd. His real estate therefore consisted of the properties now owned by John Y. Latta, Joseph C. Boyd, the late William Armstrong, and the late John Boyd, and contained altogether over five hundred acres.

The first meeting-house at this place stood a little west of the middle of the present graveyard. The eastern wall ran along about where Rev. Adam Boyd and Rev. William Foster are buried. It was a log structure, about thirty-five or forty feet square. The first notice we have of it is at the ordination of Mr. Boyd, in October, 1724, when the Presbytery, as recorded in their minutes, met for that purpose "at Ackterara meeting-house," and on which occasion Mr. Gillespie made the proclamation already referred to "at the door of the meeting-house." As the congregation had supplies from the year 1720, the probabilities are that this log meeting-house was erected about the latter year, or soon thereafter, and that

David Evans and Daniel Macgill preached in it previous to Mr. Boyd.

It was the custom of the Presbyterian emigrants, wherever they formed a settlement, as soon as they had reared or obtained dwellings for their families, to organize congregations and erect houses of worship. These buildings were universally called "meeting-houses." The use of the term "church" for the house of worship is, among Presbyterians, an innovation of quite modern date. Presbyterians in the olden time did not go to *church*—they went to *meeting*. Indeed, in my boyhood days—and, in my estimation at least, they are not so very far in the past—I always went to *meeting*. The inquiry on Sunday morning usually was, Who is going to meeting to-day? Now, however, like the rest of the Presbyterians, I go to *church*. I am old fogy enough to wish that the term used by our fathers had been retained, but as there is not much probability that it will ever be restored, I suppose there is nothing for me, and those who, like me, are somewhat wedded to the things of the past, to do but to submit gracefully, and be carried along with the current.

This log meeting-house, after being used for a number of years, was, tradition says, accidentally burned.

The congregation then erected their second church building. It was placed a short distance northwest from where the old one had stood, and was the eastern half of the edifice torn down in 1840, when the house in which we now worship was erected. Its dimensions were about thirty-five by forty-two feet. The pulpit was in the north end, and faced the door, which was in the centre of the south wall. Many of you will remember where this door stood. It was walled up when the building was subsequently enlarged, but the mark was distinctly visible.

I cannot give the date of the erection of this second house. Corner-stones (so called) containing historical data, were not laid in those days, and no written memorial is extant, but it was some time prior to the middle of the last century. At the same time, a stone session house, fifteen by twenty feet, was erected in the rear of the church. This building is still standing in the north-west corner of the present graveyard. It has an age of over a century and a quarter, and it is hoped that the trustees will preserve it as a memorial of the past. In early times it was very common to have these session houses—study houses they used to be styled—in connection with every meeting-house. I well remember hearing the term "study house" applied to this building in my young days. They were designed for the use of the ministers and elders of the church. Candidates for admission to church privileges were there examined. The ministers were accustomed to use them in preparing for the services, when they arrived before the hour at which they began, and they would also resort to them to prepare for the afternoon service.

The bounds of the congregation were curtailed on its southern side, by the formation of a new congregation about the year 1730, at Fagg's Manor, in Londonderry township. That church was originally called New Londonderry, and bore that name for some years. The name of Fagg's Manor was subsequently given to it from the circumstance that it is situated in the north-west corner of a tract of land containing about seven thousand acres, which had been granted by William Penn to his daughter Letitia Aubrey, and called Fagg's Manor in honor of Sir John Fagg, a relative of the Penn family. The new congregation, although efforts were made at an early date to obtain a minister from the Associate Presbytery in Scotland, was without a pastor until the year 1739, fifteen years after Boyd came to Octorara, when the gifted Samuel Blair settled among them. The next year, a great revival of religion commenced there, which appears to have continued for a number of years. That church has a very interesting history, which it is hoped some Old Mortality will unearth, and set in order, at no distant day.

In the year 1732, the Presbytery of New Castle was divided, and the Presbytery of Donegal formed from the western portion of its territory. Upper Octorara was set off to the new Presbytery, and belonged to it until the year 1755, when it was retransferred to New Castle, of which it continued to be a member until the recent formation of the Presbytery of Chester, to which it now belongs.

At an early date, an extensive settlement of Scotch-Irish Presbyterians had been made in the neighborhood of what is usually called Brandywine Manor, then called, and ever since officially known as the "Forks of Brandywine." Those people formed a part of the congregation of Upper Octorara, and came to this place to worship, some of them coming a distance of over ten miles.

At a meeting of the Presbytery of Donegal, held at Octorara Church June 5th, 1734, they make this record:

"The people on the Forks of Brandywine, being a part of Mr. Boyd's congregation, put in a supplication to the Presbytery for liberty of erecting a meeting house for Mr. Boyd to preach in, when sometimes he comes to them, which was granted."

Again, when the Presbytery of Donegal met, on the 4th day of April, 1735, they say:

"A supplication from the people on the Forks of Brandywine was presented and read; wherein they suppose themselves to be a distinct erected congregation of people by Presbyterial authority, and desiring supplies accordingly." "And also, another from the elders of the congregation of Octorara, desiring the subscription of those persons belonging to said people, may be continued to Mr. Boyd's support."

The Presbytery, having these contending applications, were no little perplexed. But they eventually came to the conclusion, "that the people on the Forks of Brandywine committed an error in supposing that they were already recognized as an independent congregation; expressing at the same time their conviction that such a measure would soon be expedient, if not indispensable, as leave had already been given them to build a house for their more convenient enjoying the visits of Mr. Boyd."

At the next meeting of Presbytery, a supplication from the people of the Forks of Brandywine was presented and read, the substance of which was, that they might be erected into a distinct congregation, and that Presbytery would concur with them in endeavoring to obtain a visit from some of those young gentlemen lately from Ireland, and who have joined the Presbytery of New Castle, in order to their consulting about giving such minister a call."

The Presbytery, after some hesitation, granted their request; and, on the 18th of September, 1735, erected them into a separate congregation, and they accordingly, at that date, ceased to be an integral part of Octorara. They called as their pastor the Rev. Samuel Black, who was ordained and installed November 10th, 1736. Mr. Black continued in that connection for a few years, when he was either suspended or deposed from the gospel ministry.

About this period, differences arose in the Presbyterian Church, which culminated in what was called "the great schism," by which the church was rent in twain, and remained thus divided from 1741 to 1758, a period of seventeen years. This division was not the result of any difference between the parties on doctrinal sentiments—for both agreed in the cordial adoption of the confession of faith and catechisms—but of opinion as to certain measures connected with the great revival of 1740, which revival extended from Massachusetts to Georgia, and in which Whitefield, the Tennants, Samuel Blair and others were prominent actors.

On the subject of this great revival, the ministers of the Synod of Philadelphia were divided.

The friends of Whitefield and the revival regarded all who opposed them as setting themselves in opposition to the glorious work of grace, and as enemies of God, and uncharitably condemned them as unconverted men and hypocrites. On the other hand, the opposers of the revival, as they were called, disclaimed all opposition to it, but censured the kind of preaching adopted by those who claimed to be its friends, and the extravagant measures employed for promoting it. They were also offended at what they deemed the harsh and uncharitable spirit with which they were denounced and, as they said, misrepresented by the preachers on the other side.

Another cause for alienation arose from measures adopted by the Synod to prevent the admission of uneducated men into the ministry, and in regard to itinerant preaching. These were denounced by the Revivalists, who refused to be governed by them, and persisted in intruding themselves into settled congregations, and causing dissensions between the pastors and their people.

Both parties were undoubtedly to some extent in the wrong,—the old side, in setting themselves in opposition to the revival of religion, and the new side, in doing and saying many unadvised things under the influence of a fervid zeal.

The result of this contention was of course disastrous, and as already observed, ended in the dismemberment of the Church, and its division into two parties, known respectively as the "old side" and the "new side." Those who adhered to the new side, withdrew from the Synod of Philadelphia, and formed a new synod called the Synod of New York. The new side members of the Presbyteries of New Castle and Donegal also withdrew from their respective Presbyteries, and formed a new one, called "The Second Presbytery of New Castle."

This unfortunate controversy ran a plough share, as it were, through this congregation. Mr. Boyd (the pastor), and a portion of the congregation adhered to the old side. The new side members—who composed a large majority—withdrew and organized "the Second Congregation of Upper Octorara," leaving the pastor, and the minority who adhered to him, in undisputed possession of the church property. This occurred in 1741. This second congregation, after their secession, worshiped for a time in a board tent which they erected on these church grounds, a short distance north of the meeting-house, but they soon took measures for the erection of a new church, and for this purpose took out a warrant from the Proprietaries on the 10th of February, 1743, in the name of Hugh Cowan, John Robb and John Henderson, for twenty-five acres of vacant land lying on the hill north of the late residence of Cyrus Cooper, and in the same year erected thereon, near its south-east corner, a frame meeting-house, about thirty-five by forty feet, and a stone session-house, and also enclosed a grave yard.

They had supplies from the Second Presbytery of New Castle until the year 1747, when the Rev. Andrew Sterling was ordained by that Presbytery, and installed as their pastor.

The leading families in this new church were the Hamills, Boggs, Cowans, Sloans, Glendennings, Kyles, Sharps, Dickeys, Moodys, Wilsons, Kerrs, Summerills, Robbs, Hendersons, Sandfords, Allisons and others.

The spot where this New Side church stood, which is now quite retired and somewhat difficult of access, was then as public as the location of the old church, the roads at that early date being differently located from what they are at the present day. Then, the leading public road from the Pequea Valley towards Philadelphia,—using the names of the present or late owners for facility of description—came by the late residence of Martin Armstrong, near the location of the present road to where it intersects the Lancaster turnpike, thence in the same general direction diagonally across the Latta farm, passing a short distance west of the present mansion, then by this church near where the road passes at present, to a point a short distance below the residence of Oliver P. Wilson, thence, leaving the present road where it makes a curve to the right, it continued the same general course across the Wilson farm and through the woods south of it, through the twenty-five acres belonging to the new church, and passed diagonally down the hill into the valley, a short distance east of the late residence of Cyrus Cooper, from thence it continued its course down the valley, crossing Buck Run near the culvert on the Pennsylvania Railroad, and passing a short distance from Major Pomeroy's barn. The route of this old road is, in places, very perceptible, and those of you who may have curiosity enough to trace it, as I had, can very readily do so. There is a spring on the Cooper farm near to which this road passed, and tradition says, that the wagoners used frequently to stop there to water their horses and refresh themselves. The new meeting-house stood near to this road, which is spoken of in old records, as "The Meeting-house Road."

Another road ran on the brow of the hill from the neighborhood of the present village of Parkesburg, which was used by the people going to the new house from that direction, and another road led northward from near the graveyard, towards the late residence of William Parke.

The two meeting-houses, the old and the new, were about one mile distant from each other.

About the year 1740, Messrs. John Filson, William Hanna, Francis Boggs, James Blelock and others, members of Upper Octorara residing in East Fallowfield township and vicinity, and who sympathized with the New Side, erected a house of worship at Doe Run on the Strasburg road, in that township, and were organized into a congregation under the name of the "Doe Run Presbyterian Church." They had supplies from the New Side Presbytery of New Castle, until about the year 1747, when the Rev. Andrew Sterling became their pastor, in connection with the Second Congregation of Octorara.

About the year 1743, the Rev. George Whitefield, in the course of his visitations to the churches in this county, preached at Doe Run, and also at the New Side Church of Upper Octorara. There was a large board tent at Octorara, which stood on the brow of the hill a short distance west of the graveyard, in which he preached. His voice was very strong, and it is said, he could be distinctly heard at Thomas Trumans—where the late Cyrus Cooper resided.

Mr. Sterling was the pastor of these two churches until the year 1765,—a period of about eighteen years. As a preacher, he is said to have possessed much power; but he was of an impetuous disposition and very much disposed to have his own way, and in the later years of his ministry he was frequently involved in difficulties with his session and the people of his congregations. In 1761, he was complained of for not calling his session together more frequently, and consulting them in regard to the affairs of the church; for not being more thorough and regular in catechizing the congregations, and also for refusing to make proper settlements with the people, that they might know how much of his stipend was unpaid.

The Presbytery met at his church at Octorara on several occasions to adjust these difficulties, with but ill success. He became very deaf, and this, with his growing infirmities, was his excuse for not being more attentive to his duties, and for neglecting to attend the meetings of the judicatories of the Church.

At length, he was arraigned before Presbytery on account of some occurrences not necessary to be detailed here, and on the 24th of April, 1765, was deposed from the office of the ministry.

He resided within the bounds of the congregation of Doe Run, and died in West Marlborough township in August. 1765. about four months after his deposition. He was married, but left no descendants. I can give no account of his relations, except that a brother, James Sterling, was concerned in the settlement of his estate. He was a native of Ireland.

After his deposition, the churches to which he had ministered asked for supplies, and the Rev. John Blair of Faggs Manor, and Rev. John Carmichael of the Forks of Brandywine, were appointed to visit them in that capacity.

The Rev. Adam Boyd, having, as already observed, been deserted by a majority of his congregation, accepted a call on the 11th of August, 1741, from the portion of the church of the Forks of Brandywine who adhered to the Old Side—that church having also been divided—and who offered him £20 for one half of his time. From this period until the year 1758, he ministered to the Old Side portions of both Upper Octorara and the Forks of Brandywine. giving to each, one half of his time. In the latter year. the two branches at Brandywine united, and his pastoral relation to that church was dissolved. He continued to be the pastor of the Old Side Congregation at

Octorara, they, from the time his connection with Brandywine ceased, paying him for two thirds of his time.

The division in the church at large, which had existed since 1741, was healed in the year 1758, and the two bodies became one. The First and Second Presbyteries of New Castle were united, and Mr. Boyd, who had theretofore, since its formation in 1732, been a member of Donegal Presbytery, was joined to New Castle.

The First and Second Congregations of Octorara, however, continued to remain distinct congregations for a period of ten years after the union of the Synods, although many of the members of the Second Church returned to the First Church during this period.

On the 19th of January, 1768, the Second Congregation of Upper Octorara, and the congregation at Doe Run, which had together been under the pastoral care of Mr. Sterling, united in calling the Rev. William Foster, who had been licensed by the Presbytery of New Castle on the 21st of April, 1767, and had supplied their pulpits a portion of the intervening period. The call was placed in his hands by the Presbytery, and held by him under consideration.

At a meeting of Presbytery held April 20, 1768, Mr. Boyd represented his inability to minister to his people as formerly, by reason of feeble health, and requested as many supplies for his pulpit as could reasonably be granted.

Soon after this, measures were taken for the coalition of the two congregations. Mr. Boyd's people, with his approbation, harmoniously concurred in the call already extended to Mr. Foster by the other congregation; the calls were accepted by Mr. Foster, and on the 19th of October, 1768, he was duly ordained and installed as pastor of the "United Congregation of Upper Octorara," and also of the congregation of Doe Run, giving to the latter one-fourth of his time. The Rev. Robert Smith, of Pequea, presided at the ordination,—Mr. Boyd being present, and taking part in the services.

Mr. Boyd's pastoral relation was not formally dissolved, and the congregation agreed to pay him £25 yearly, during his life. He survived however but a little over a month, and died Nov. 23, 1768, at the age of seventy-six years; forty-four of which he was pastor of this church. He was buried in yonder graveyard—tradition says—on the spot where the pulpit of the log church stood, in which he preached during the early part of his ministry. His widow survived till November 9, 1779. The stone covering his remains records, that he was "eminent through life for modest piety, diligence in his office, prudence, equanimity and peace."

He was a man of great exactness, and kept an account book full of minute memoranda, commencing in 1741, and extending down to his last days. In those times, the minister collected his stipends himself, and in this volume, he records the payments of each subscriber, whether in money, produce or otherwise, with the offsets, the times of their death or removal, and the attending circumstances. His salary was not large. During a part of his ministry, it did not exceed £30 from this congregation, and at no time, did it much, if any, exceed £60. This was doubtless added to by the other congregations, which from time to time he had under his charge.

The circumstances of the people were limited, and while they could not contribute largely to his support, they seem to have been uniformly commendable in fulfilling their promises, and several remembered him in their dying testaments by small bequests.

In his preparation for the pulpit, he used a sort of short-hand. The book I have referred to, contains several of his sermons thus written.

He was accustomed to visit the families of his congregation, and as the roads in those days, were to some extent mere bridle-paths, and riding vehicles had not come into use, he frequently made these journeys on foot. On such occasions—at least in his later days—he carried a cane, which has been preserved in the family, and has been handed down from father to son, in one branch of his descendants to the present time, and which, through the kindness of the present possessors of it, I am permitted to exhibit to you to-day. The lower part, as you will see, is somewhat worn—caused, it is said, by his striking it through the crusted snow. As he died in 1768, one hundred and two years ago, this cane has an age of probably a century and a quarter.

An instance of Mr. Boyd's honesty has been transmitted—that having a horse, fine looking, but unruly, he took him to a neighboring vendue to sell;

the cryer began to praise him, and set off his good properties, much in the modern style, but the old gentleman rebuked him, saying it was not so, that if he had been such a horse, he never would have thought of parting with him; and told the bidders the faults of the animal, and the occasion of his offering him for sale.

Adam Boyd left five sons and six daughters. The eldest, John, is said to have been licensed to preach, and to have died young. Thomas settled on a plantation conveyed to him by his father, embracing the eastern portion of his lands already referred to, adjoining this church property on the north, and which —now divided into two farms—is still in the possession of his descendants.

Andrew remained upon the homestead; was active during the war of the revolution, held a commission as Colonel, and was for a time Lieutenant of the county of Chester. His duties in this office, were, to call out, equip and forward troops as they were needed, and to have the general oversight within the county, of supplying and sustaining the army in the field. His appointment to such a position shows the estimation in which he was held. He died March 23, 1786, at the age of forty-six years. Among his descendants, are Rev. Andrew Boyd Cross, of Baltimore, and the widow of the late Rev. Richard Webster, of Mauch Chunk.

Adam, another son, resided in Wilmington, North Carolina, and commenced the "Cape Fear Mercury," in October, 1767. He was a true friend of liberty, and was a leading member of the "Committee of Safety." In 1776, he exchanged the press for the pulpit, and was chaplain of the North Carolina brigade.

Samuel, the youngest son, entered Mr. McDowell's school at Elk, in the summer of 1760, and became a student in the College of Philadelphia in 1764. He entered on the practice of medicine and removed to Virginia.

Of the daughters of Rev. Adam Boyd, Margaret married the Rev. Joseph Tate; Janet, the Rev. Robert McMordrie; and Agnes, the Rev. Samson Smith.

His marriage-portions to his daughters were large, according to the notions of that day, and show the thoughtfulness, as well as the liberality of the parents;—thus, on the marriage of his eldest daughter, he gave her, besides a silk gown, a bed and its furniture, a horse and saddle, and nearly every article for housekeeping, all of which are carefully entered in his book.

How he managed to raise a family of five sons and six daughters, with the small stipend he received, and on a poor farm, in the condition agriculture was in at that time; educating two of his sons for the ministry, and one as a physician, and giving to each of his other sons a large plantation, besides portions to his daughters, is more than I can divine. I imagine there are few in our day that could do it. It is true, that money was more valuable then than now, but not so much so as we might suppose, as many of the necessaries of life commanded more than they do at the present day.

The union of the two branches of Octorara under one pastorate, does not appear, at first, to have been with the entire concurrence of the New Side. Some of them refused for a time, to worship with the united congregation, and received therefor the censure of the Presbytery. They gradually however, in time, became reconciled to the new order of things.

One of the first acts of the united congregation, was to obtain patents from the proprietaries for the lands belonging to them, and which had theretofore been held by warrant and survey. A warrant had been taken out by the Rev. Adam Boyd, dated May 25, 1743, for the lands occupied by the congregation of which he was pastor, and a survey made in pursuance thereof. A patent was granted for these lands on the 26th of April, 1769, to the Rev. William Foster, William Clingan, Hugh Cowan and John Fleming, they having been designated by the congregation to receive a patent and to hold the same, as expressed therein, "for the purpose of erecting and continuing a church or house of religious worship, for the use of the united congregation at Octorara, in Sadsbury township, and their descendants and successors, in such manner as the majority of the congregation shall, from time to time, order, direct and appoint." The tract—according to the patent—contains nine acres and one hundred and thirty-eight perches, and allowance—the actual contents, according to a more recent survey, being eleven acres and fifty perches—and is the one now occupied by the congregation.*

* See Appendix C.

CHURCH EDIFICE, ERECTED IN 1769.

The tract of twenty-five acres and allowance on the north valley hill, for which a warrant had been granted to Hugh Cowan, John Robb and John Henderson, on the 10th of February, 1743, for the use of the New Side portion of Octorara, and survey thereof made January 30, 1744, was, by direction of the united congregation, patented on the 7th of June, 1769, to Joseph Cowan and Hugh Cowan, "in trust to and for the use of the United Congregation of Presbyterians at Octorara."

In those days, when lands were taken up, names were frequently given to them. Accordingly, the tract on which this church stands, was patented by the name of "Union,"—probably in commemoration of the union of the two congregations,—and the twenty-five acre tract was called "Fellowship."

The union of the congregations, rendered it necessary that they should have increased accommodations for public worship, neither of their houses having sufficient capacity, and accordingly about the year 1769, they proceeded to enlarge the house on the grounds of the first congregation, by extending it westward about thirty-five feet, thus making it in size, about forty-two by seventy feet. In this extension, they simply used the north, east, and south walls of the old building—the floor, roof, and every other part being entirely new—so that the enlarged building was substantially a new one, and was the third meeting-house erected on these grounds.

In an old document in my possession, speaking of this building, it is stated that "when the first and second congregations united into one body, they built a large and convenient stone church on the grounds of the first congregation. the ancient place from the first settlement of the gospel in this part of the country."

The carpenter work was probably done by Samuel McClellan, the ancestor of the present family of that name in this congregation, who had removed into this township from Newtown township. Delaware County, about the year 1763, and settled where his grandson James L. McClellan, now resides. He was a joiner by trade, but did carpenter work. It is certain that he built the pews. He would make as many at a time as his shop would conveniently hold, and then haul them to the church and put them up. On one occasion, while he was thus engaged, his shop took fire and was burned, and with it about £60 worth of work, besides the materials.

It may be interesting to describe this third church building more minutely, as it was the one in which our fathers worshipped for many years, and for its day, was one of more than ordinary elegance.

The building—as already observed—was about seventy feet in length from east to west, and about forty-two in width from north to south. The south wall—which was the front of the building—was what is called range work, pointed with black or dark colored mortar, and then penciled white, and as I recollect it, presented a very fine appearance. The walls were about sixteen feet in height to the square, and twenty feet to the centre of the ceiling, which was arched. There were three doors of entrance for the congregation; the main one, in the centre of the south side, and one in each end, east and west. The south door had over it a heavy cornice. The windows were large, arched, and had very small panes of glass. The pulpit stood on the north side, facing the south or main door. An aisle, some seven or eight feet wide, ran the length of the church from east to west, about one-third of the distance across the room from the north side, and another wide aisle from the main door to this cross-aisle. There were also two small blind aisles, as they might be termed, running from the east and west aisle to the south wall. The number of pews was fifty-eight. There were four rows facing the north or pulpit side, with seven pews in each, and on each side of the pulpit there were twelve pews, extending from the long aisle to the north wall. Those on each side of the aisle running from the main door, and those on the north side of the east and west aisle, were quite long, and were frequently occupied by two families. There were also six square pews, three on each side of the church, against the east and west walls, and south of the long aisle. They were entered from the blind aisles referred to. All the pews had high perpendicular backs, in accordance with the notion of the times. The pulpit—a neat piece of workmanship for that day—was square and closed, and would hold three persons. It stood quite high, although not so much so as the most of pulpits of that day, and was surmounted by a huge sounding board. A small door opened into the closed space underneath it. The pulpit was painted white; the pews were unpainted.

In front of the pulpit there was a large square pew, with seats around three sides of it. This was called the elders' pew, and on communion Sabbaths, and sometimes on other occasions, it was occupied by them. The precentor, or *clerk*, as he was usually called, had his seat there, and it was also frequently occupied by persons whose hearing was dull.

In addition to the outer doors referred to, there was a small door on the north side, more especially designed for the convenience of the minister, which opened into a double pew, on the west side of the pulpit, and out of which pew the stairs led to the pulpit. There was a window over this door, from which the pulpit was lighted.

A table stood in the elders' pew, which on communion occasions was placed in the long aisle in front of the pulpit, and the communion elements placed upon it. This table—a relic of the past, and having an age of over one hundred years—has been preserved, and may now be seen in the lecture room of this church. It is forty-eight inches long, and twenty-nine inches wide.

The communion was administered in the long aisle, at tables, on each side of which the communicants seated themselves.

After the completion of the new building, the united congregation agreed to sell twenty-four acres of the Fellowship tract, reserving two acres and a half in the southeast corner, (being the remaining acre and the allowance of six per cent.,) on which were the meeting-house, session-house, and graveyard. The trustees, who held the title of the lands, disregarded the wishes of the congregation in this respect, and sold and conveyed to James Sharp, by deed dated 22d December, 1769, all of said tract, except a piece in the southeast corner, six and a half perches by twelve perches. A controversy arose about the matter, which was referred to six of the members of the adjoining congregations of Faggs Manor and Forks of Brandywine for settlement. The difficulties were finally adjusted, on the recommendation of the referees, by James Sharp re-conveying to the trustees the surplus over the twenty-four acres intended to be sold. This reconveyance was made May 8, 1772. The proceeds of the lands thus sold to Sharp were applied to liquidate the debt incurred in erecting the new church.

The congregation subsequently sold all of the reserved lands, except about one-fourth of an acre, including the burial ground, the title to which remains in this church.

The frame meeting-house was sold to Joseph Park, Esq., in the year 1772, and removed by him to where the barn now stands, on the property lately owned by Evan Jones, and was used for purposes connected with the tannery for some years. It gradually went to decay, and soon after the year 1811, was torn down.

The stone session-house was used for some time as

a tenement by the owners of the land on which it stood, but it has long since disappeared.

The only remaining landmark to designate this interesting spot is the graveyard. That is about twenty-five yards square, and is enclosed with a substantial stone wall. It contains nineteen headstones, recording the deaths of twenty-three persons, and there are graves with nothing to tell who is resting therein. Indeed, the yard appears to be pretty well filled. The oldest memorial is that of Joseph Wilson, who died in the year 1751.*

These old burial grounds which are no longer used, are so generally neglected and suffered to go to decay, that it is pleasing to observe that *this* is an exception, and that it has recently received proper attention at the hands of the trustees. The ancestors of many of the present members of this and neighboring churches lie there, and their descendants should guard their dust with jealous care.

I would also in this connection suggest to the trustees of this church the propriety of erecting a simple memorial stone to mark the site of the old frame meeting-house. I am sure the present proprietor of the lands will cordially give his assent. It stood a short distance northwest of the graveyard, and its location can now be readily pointed out. In a few years, all knowledge of it will have passed from the minds of men.

The Rev. William Foster was born in Little Britain township, Lancaster county, in 1740. He was of

* See Appendix I.

Scotch-Irish stock, and son of Alexander Foster, who had removed from the County Derry, in the north of Ireland, some years before, and settled in that township. He was graduated at the College of New Jersey in 1764, having for his cotemporaries in that institution David Ramsay, the historian, Judge Jacob Rush, Oliver Ellsworth, Nathaniel Niles, and Luther Martin. He was taken under the care of the Presbytery of New Castle as a probationer for the ministry, October 23, 1766, and, as already observed, was licensed by that Presbytery April 21, 1767.

He was a very popular preacher from the first, as is evidenced by the fact that at the next meeting of Presbytery after his licensure, the congregations of Upper Octorara 2d, Doe Run, Bethel, and Faggs Manor, all of which were without pastors, in requesting supplies, asked, as expressed in the minutes of Presbytery, "particularly for Mr. Foster." In a short time thereafter, he had in his hands three calls, one from Upper Octorara and Doe Run; another from Faggs Manor, then recently vacant by the removal of Rev. John Blair to Princeton; and a third from White Clay Creek and Head of Christina. He accepted the first, and was installed October 19, 1768, being then about twenty-eight years of age.

Soon after his licensure, he married Hannah, a daughter of Rev. Samuel Blair, formerly of Faggs Manor, and a grand-daughter of Lawrence Van Hook, Esq., formerly one of the judges of the Court of Common Pleas of New York, who was among the first settlers from the United Netherlands.

In December, 1770, Mr. Foster purchased from John Dickey a farm containing about two hundred and fifty acres, to which he removed, and where he resided during his life. The mansion house which he occupied was that now belonging to the family of the late William Parke, a short distance east of this church.

In the Revolution, Mr. Foster engaged heartily in the cause of civil liberty, and encouraged all who heard him to do their utmost in defence of their rights. In the beginning of 1776, he preached a very patriotic and stirring sermon to the young men of his congregation and neighborhood upon the subject of their duty to their country, in its then trying situation. One of the young men who heard this discourse was Joseph McClellan, the fire of whose patriotism was so kindled that he at once resolved to engage in the service of his country; and, by the intervention of Mr. Foster and some other friends, he received a lieutenant's commission, and joined the army. Many of the older members of this congregation will remember him in after life as Colonel Joseph McClellan, a patriot, a professing Christian, and an upright man, and of whose honored name his descendants may be justly proud. His wife was Kezia, a daughter of Joseph Park, and among his descendants were Joseph Hemphill and Colonel Thomas S. Bell, Jr., members of the Chester County Bar, the last of whom lost his life in 1862, while gallantly leading his regiment at the battle of Antietam.

On one occasion, Mr. Foster was called to Lancaster

to preach to troops collected there previous to their joining the main army. The discourse was so acceptable that it was printed and circulated, and did much to arouse the spirit of patriotism among the people.

Indeed, the Presbyterian clergymen generally were staunch Whigs, and contributed greatly to keep alive the flame of liberty, which our disasters had frequently caused to be well nigh extinguished in the long and unequal contest; and but for them, it would often have been impossible to obtain recruits to keep up the forces requisite to oppose a too often victorious enemy. Some of them lost their lives, and others were driven from their congregations, in consequence of their zeal in behalf of their country.

It was a great object with the British officers to silence the Presbyterian preachers as far as possible, and with this view they frequently despatched parties of light horse into the country to surprise and take prisoners unsuspecting clergymen.

An expedition of this kind was planned against Mr. Foster. When he preached to his congregation at Doe Run, which was about eight miles distant from Octorara, it was his custom always to go on Saturday and return on Monday. One Sabbath afternoon he was seen returning home, which gave alarm to the family, they conjecturing that something very unusual either had taken place, or was about to happen. It turned out that he had received information that morning at Doe Run that a party of British light horse were to leave Wilmington in the evening, to take him prisoner and burn Upper Octorara church. The neighbors collected and removed his family and library to houses remote from the public road.

The information he had received was correct. An expedition was actually sent by Sir William Howe for that purpose. After proceeding, however, about twelve miles on their way, they were informed by a tory tavern keeper that their purpose was known, and that a few miles further on, parties of militia were stationed to intercept them; on hearing which they returned to Wilmington without having accomplished their object.

Mr. Foster died on the 30th of September, 1780, at the age of forty years, having been pastor of this church, in connection with Doe Run, about twelve years. He had been preaching, and on his walk home was overtaken by a heavy rain, which brought on the attack that terminated his life.

He was a brother-in-law of the Rev. John Carmichael, at that time pastor of the church of Forks of Brandywine. The Rev. Dr. Robert Smith, of Pequea, was an uncle of Mrs. Foster, he having married a sister of Mrs. Foster's father, the Rev. Samuel Blair. Soon after Mr. Foster's death, Mr. Carmichael addressed a letter to Dr. Smith, containing a statement of his religious exercises during his last illness. This letter is so interesting, and portrays so fully the beloved character of Mr. Foster that I am sure you will pardon me for presenting it to you. It reads thus:

Rev. and Dear Sir:—

As you were abroad a considerable distance on important business at the time of the sickness and much lamented death of my dear brother-in-law, the Rev. William Foster, and since you have been informed that he left this world in a very happy frame of mind, and you wish to know the particulars, and what I heard him say with his dying lips on his death-bed, I very readily comply with your desire; for notwithstanding the subject is in itself melancholy, yet I bless God I have it in my power to send you such an account of the blessed and unusually happy state of his precious soul in his sickness, and at his dissolution, as cannot fail to be refreshing to every one that loves our Lord Jesus Christ in sincerity; for, "blessed are the dead who die in the Lord."

As soon as I heard of his illness, I went to see him, and, from the bad color of his skin and heavy fever, I was afraid the consequence might prove fatal. But Mr. Foster himself did not apprehend much danger. After much conversation, and after we had prayed together, I returned home, and in a few days heard he was worse, which I indeed much feared would be the case. I went to see him again, and was alarmed to find his disease had increased much during the short time of my absence. I told him my fear, that he would be taken from us; while at the same time I felt much difficulty in being resigned to such a step of divine providence, as both church and state needed the exercise of his valuable talents. Mr. Foster said he was more apprehensive that his disorder might terminate in his dissolution than at first; but said he, "The will of God be done. Whatever my great Master God and Saviour Jesus Christ does is right; and blessed be his name, I am not afraid to meet death."

We entered into a free conversation on the state of religion in our own and the neighboring churches around us. Mr. Foster observed, that although his own pastoral charges and the congregations contiguous were no doubt in a declining state of religion, and did just now partake of the present declension of the day; yet we ought to bless God it was no worse with us than it was, when we consider how much the divine influence of God, the Holy Spirit, is withdrawn from the means of grace in general, and the many and strange temptations which these times throw in the way of real piety and true holiness. He said that his people, considered as a congregation, were both solemn and attentive in time of public worship, and discovered much affection to him as their pastor; that he felt in himself much outgoing of Christian love and affection to them: that in his public labors in his Divine Master's service, both at home and abroad, he had much greater freedom and enlargement of soul in the real things of God and eternal life than usual; which was exceedingly refreshing to him, so that he found himself really fed with divine things, while he was breaking the bread of life to others; and that this had been his happy case for some time past.

I then returned home, full of fears that Mr. Foster would soon be removed from us by death; and I found that there was too much cause for my fears, as a messenger was sent to request me to come and see him, as he was supposed to be near his end. I came, but as too much company weakened him, I did not go in where he lay, or let him know I was come. But after a little, being sensible that his dissolution was near, I was anxious to see him, and converse with him about affairs of infinite moment, as he was on the verge of eternity, and in the full exercise of his rational powers.

I therefore desired Mrs. Foster to tell my dear brother that I was come. He was glad to hear it, and desired to see me. I was much affected to see him so much reduced in his outward man, attended with so many evidences of the near approach of death. He took me very affectionately by the hand, and held it. I said to him, inasmuch as you are too weak to speak much, I wish you only to answer the few questions I will ask you, by a sign, or yes or no, or a word or two, as you feel yourself able.

I asked him, as you are now on the very brink of the eternal world, and in a few hours to appear before the great God, to answer for the deeds done in the body, how do you feel in your soul, and what are your hopes of eternal life? He answered, that although it was very difficult for him to speak much, yet he would do all in his power for the best of Masters, in leaving testimony for him and his precious truths with his last breath, and would not have us stop him from speaking, although it might seem to hurt him. "What I shall say," he said, "you may depend on as sincere and from the heart, as I can be under no temptation to deceive; for I am a dying man, and now die in the full belief of the truth and vast importance of those doctrines of grace which I have been preaching to mankind, and I do now with my dying breath give my testimony to them as true. I am venturing my soul on their veracity with the greatest cheerfulness; and adored be my God and Saviour for it. I do now feel, on this my death-bed, their application by the blessed spirit to my soul. I do find, by a most inexpressible experience, that while my outward man is decaying, my inward man is gathering strength every moment; and the nearer my approach to death and eternity, the greater my joy, insomuch that I find all those sweet, precious promises of eternal life dispersed through the holy, dear book of God harmonizing for my divine consolation, by the spirit's application of them to my soul. And I now feed on them by faith, so that I am not able to tell the thousandth part of the joy and evangelical consolation, and real comfort my soul feels, and which has been increasing in my heart since the beginning of this sickness, even to this hour, like a stream of the water of the river of life flowing in a growing tide to my soul. Oh! how shall I praise and sufficiently adore my God, my Saviour and my Jesus, my all and in all!" He then paused, and I asked him if he had not at times some fears and doubts lest his heart should deceive him in this great eternal affair. He replied "In my early days, and in my youth, under the gospel, I had many alarms and awful fears through the conviction I then had of the natural badness of my heart; and the more powerful and clear the sermon I heard, the more I was convinced of my undone state by nature. But I had a great desire to be a preacher of the precious gospel of Jesus Christ to the world; yet felt an exceedingly great terror at times, more especially lest I should preach an unknown Christ. I importuned heaven to save me from such a judgment; and forever adored be the Lord Jesus Christ, my divine Master, for he was pleased to answer my prayers. He was graciously pleased to reveal himself in a saving manner to my soul, so that, after the experience of a number of years, I have reason to know with much gospel confidence, that what I called my convictions at the time of my soul's closure with Christ, and the very solemn exercise of my heart, was not a delusion, but a great reality. I have not been preaching an unknown Christ. I know in whom I have believed, and that he is able to keep that which I have committed to him against the last day. I now tell you on my death-bed, that the divine beauty, harmony, moral excellency, and heavenly sweetness of the way of salvation for sinners of mankind through the Lord Jesus Christ, did continue to grow and increase to my view from the time of my conversion until this solemn moment." He then paused, and I asked him if he was not at times affected with the prevalency of a self-righteous spirit. He replied, that he found that spirit at times a very sore enemy to keep in subjection, but that just now he happily found himself enabled to rest wholly on the Lord Jesus Christ and his righteousness; and he felt himself so happily relieved from the enemy as to be full of joy and divine consolation. I then asked him which he would choose, if it was at his option just now, either to live or die. He answered, that he had no choice to make: God's choice was his; so that he could say from the heart, "Thy will be done on earth as it is in heaven." If the King of Zion chose to continue him longer on earth to serve him, he would say, Amen; and would wish to preach again to souls, as one from the dead; but to depart and be with Christ was far better. There was nothing on earth worth enjoying compared to the heavenly glories, and death was but the partition wall between God's children and infinite happiness, suited to the nature of an immortal soul. All that the earth calls good and great, with all its possible splendor, is but dust in the balance when put in competition with divine things, and viewed in the light of eternity, as he now viewed them; and all their false appearances vanish as darkness before the rising day of the glory of Immanuel's land. He then said, "Oh! how sweet is the gospel of Jesus Christ and its divine truths just now to my soul." He then paused, and I asked him if he did not find it difficult to part with his dear wife and little children. He answered, that the ties of nature were very binding, and their dissolution hard to be borne, but that the God of nature had a right to rend those bonds and ties, how or when he pleased. Death, said he, must separate us some time, and God's time is the best. I have no fear but God will take care of my widow and my fatherless children. God tells me, in Jeremiah xlix. 11, "Leave thy fatherless children; I will preserve them alive; and let thy widows trust in me." This is like a bill of exchange put into my hand by the Great Secretary of heaven, God the Holy Ghost, to draw on the bank of heaven for the support of my family after my decease. I rely upon it, and do you think it will be protested? No, it cannot, except through infidelity on the part of the dependents, which they must guard against if they wish to be happy. I do cheerfully commit my earthly concerns of every kind into the hands of the great Messiah, Jesus Christ, who has all power in heaven and on earth; to whom I commit my soul triumphing; for I am certain that all things shall work together for good finally to God's people. Many more things he said of the same heavenly kind and strain, which showed how full his soul was of God, how empty of self, and how much his conversation was in heaven.

I then took my leave of him in the most affectionate manner, and hastened home to bring Mrs. Carmichael to see him, if she could once more in this world; but our ears were struck with the melancholy news of his death, on the road, by a messenger sent to inform us. We came to Bochim, the place of weeping; and I was told by those who were present, that his happy frame of soul continued, and even increased, to the last moments of his life. A few hours before his departure, he called Mr. Sample* to his bedside and said, "You see, my dear sir, that I am grappling with the king of terrors; and justly is he so called; for to die is indeed a solemn thing. But this is the gate by which we must enter in: and, blessed be my God, I am not afraid to pass the Jordan of death. My Joshua has gone before. Oh, how comfortable to have a God to go to in such an hour! And let me now, my dear sir, in your presence, give my testimony with my dying breath to God's truths; that it is alone in true religion that real comfort is to be found; that God's favor and loving kindness, in this trying

---

* Nathaniel W. Sample, a student of theology under his care.

hour, will be found better than life itself. Oh, sir, remember the infinite importance of the work in which you are engaged. It may appear important to you now, but when, like me, you are just launching into the world of spirits, and have eternity in full view, it will appear infinitely more so. With respect to the dear people of my charge, it would be one of the foremost things to make life desirable to have an opportunity of meeting with them once more, to declare to them the counsels of heaven with the emphasis of death and eternity on my lips, as I now feel them, and so, if possible, to press on them more closely those important realities which belong to their everlasting peace; but infinite wisdom has determined otherwise. I still hope that God has something great and good in store for Octorara: therefore, my dear sir, when I am sleeping in the dust, do you deliver this message to the dear people of my charge as the last words of their dying pastor to them, that when I was just launching into the eternal world, and had it in full view, and just appearing before their and my great, eternal, and just Judge, my conscience then bore testimony that I never had concealed from them any of the divine counsels with which I was intrusted, and which was necessary for them to know, nor had I ever delivered to them a doctrine but on the veracity of which I can venture my own salvation, and that those very important truths which I have delivered to them in life, are now the support of my soul and the foundation of my hopes. But inasmuch as infinite wisdom has denied them and me an interview until the morning of the resurrection, tell them, oh, tell them, from me, just now expiring, to prepare to have the solemn account then and there settled, before their and my God—I to answer in what manner, from what views, and from what ends I have declared the truth of the everlasting gospel to them—they to answer how they have heard those truths, and in what manner they have improved them."

As God has favored him with the full and free use of his reason through the whole of his sickness, when he found himself in the very jaws of death, lest those about him should think his suffering intolerable, and tend to lessen the idea they ought to have of God's love to his dying servants, he said, "Though my body is so wrought, do not think my burthen too hard to bear; it is not. Death is not so hard as I was wont to imagine. I can bear it. My God supports me in it." He then took leave of his dear wife and children, and other tender connections present, in the hope of meeting them in a better world, and soon after fell asleep in Jesus.

Death had now executed its office, and had rent asunder the bands which united the soul and body; the latter to rest in the grave until the morning of the resurrection; the former angels conveyed into heaven, to dwell forever with its Maker, God.

Mr. Foster was evidently a man of very superior mind, and was much esteemed and respected by all who knew him for his solid sense and unaffected piety. By his congregation, whom he had united by his zeal, talents and piety, after the schism which had for many years divided them, he was affectionately beloved, and his death, at an early age, was universally lamented. It is evident, from the minutes of Presbytery, that he was held in high estimation by his ministerial brethren, as his name constantly occurs in connection with positions of trust and responsibility. He occasionally received under his care theological students. The Rev. Nathaniel W. Sample, whose name occurs in the letter of Mr. Carmichael, which I have just read, and who was the esteemed pastor of churches in Lancaster county for forty years, was, at the time of Mr. Foster's death, one of his students.

The congregation procured a tombstone to be placed over his remains in yonder church-yard, which bears the following inscription, written by the Rev. Mr. Carmichael:

HERE LIES ENTOMBED
WHAT WAS MORTAL OF THE
Rev. Mr. WILLIAM FOSTER,
WHO DEPARTED THIS LIFE
SEPT. THE 30TH, 1780,
IN THE 41ST YEAR
OF HIS AGE.

Foster, of sense profound, flowing in eloquence,
Of aspect comely, saint without pretence,
Foster the brave, the wise, the good, thou'st gone
To reign forever with thy Saviour on his throne,
And left thy widowed charge to sit and weep alone.
If grace and gifts like thine a mortal could reprieve
From the dark regions of the dreary grave,
Thy friend, dear Shade, would ne'er inscribe thy stone,
Nor with the Church's tears have mixed his own.

Mr. Foster left eight children, four sons and four daughters, the oldest about thirteen or fourteen years, and the youngest one year of age. His will, executed the day before his death, is in the handwriting of William Clingan, Esq., an elder in this church, and a man of note, and was witnessed by Rev. John Carmichael, Nathaniel W. Sample, and Joseph Park. It contains, among others, this provision: "My son Samuel to be made a scholar." His executors were his widow, Hannah Foster, and his friends William Clingan and Matthew Boyd. The estate left by him was not large in point of value, but Mrs. Foster was a very prudent, managing woman, and, under the blessing of Providence, was enabled to raise her children until they were of an age to take care of themselves.

Mr. Foster, in his lifetime, had sold a small portion of his farm to Joseph Park, Esq., who had other property adjoining. In 1790, Mrs. Foster, as executrix, sold sixty-two acres to Mr. Park, and thirty-six acres to Thomas Truman; and in 1793, conveyed to her two oldest sons, Samuel B. Foster and Alexander W. Foster, the remainder of the land, being about one hundred and fifty acres; and they, in 1797, sold and conveyed the same to Mr. Park, who thus became the owner of the greater portion of the land originally owned by Mr. Foster.

In February, 1779, Mr. Foster had opened a classical school, and had as teacher Mr. Francis Hindman —afterwards Rev. Francis Hindman—who resided with him. This school was in operation at Mr. Foster's death, and was carried on by Mr. Hindman for about eighteen months thereafter, in all a period of three years. I mention this circumstance to show that Mr. Foster, a scholar himself, took a deep interest in thorough education, and that at that early day the classics were taught within the bounds of this congregation.

The appraisement of Mr. Foster's personal effects was made in what is known as continental currency, and amounted in that currency—then very much depreciated in value—to £26,743.

In those days, slavery existed in a mild form in Pennsylvania, and we find Negro James' time appraised at £1,200; Violet and her child at £4,200; and Negro Will at £2,700.

The library, which contained 104 volumes, besides

school books and pamphlets, was appraised at £3,004. It sold for £69 in specie. The titles of the books owned by him are given in detail in the inventory, and show that his library, for that day, was large and well selected.

In 1780, an act of Assembly was passed, providing for the gradual abolition of slavery, which required the owners of slaves to register their names and ages in the office of the clerk of the courts. In accordance with its provisions, the following registry was made by Mr. Foster:

No. 1. A negro woman named Violet, aged twenty-four years, a slave for life.

No. 2. A negro boy named Will, aged fourteen years, a slave for life.

No. 3. A female negro child, named Jean, aged one year, a slave for life.

In 1796, the entire family removed to Cussawaga, (now Meadville). Two of the sons, Samuel Blair Foster and Alexander W. Foster, became members of the bar, and were among the most eminent lawyers of western Pennsylvania, and were long recognized as the leaders of the bar in that part of the State. Alexander had been admitted to the bar of Chester county, in November, 1793, and in 1796, on his removal to Cussawaga, became agent of the Holland Land Company. He devoted half a century to the labors of his profession, and died at Mercer, in 1843. Samuel Blair Foster was the father of the Hon. Henry D. Foster of Westmoreland, and Alexander W. Foster left a son, Alexander W. Foster, Esq., who is now a prominent member of the Pittsburg bar. William B. Foster, formerly canal commissioner of this State, was a descendant of James Foster, a brother of the Rev. William Foster.

Mrs. Foster survived until the 14th of May, 1810, when she died, at the residence of a daughter, in Mercer, Pa., at the age of sixty-five years. She was distinguished for an equanimity of temper that adorned those principles in which she had been educated, and which she constantly practiced through life. She saw her approaching dissolution with a calm composure which nothing could inspire but a review of a life of piety and virtue, and full persuasion of another and better world. A singular circumstance was connected with her decease, which I will relate. On the morning of the day she died, one of her sons (Alexander) was at her bedside, and observing her lips moving, leaned down and asked her what she was saying. Her reply was, " It is singular that two sisters should enter heaven's gates upon the same day." Upon being asked to explain, she was only able to reply. " Sister Carmichael." In the course of the day she died; and after the lapse of weeks—for the mails were few in those days—the family heard for the first time of the illness and death of their aunt, the widow of Rev. John Carmichael, who had died on the same day with her sister, Mrs. Foster. I have no theory to broach with reference to the subject suggested by this incident. I simply relate the occurrence, which is well authenticated.

I have spoken of Mrs. Foster as a daughter of Rev. Samuel Blair, formerly of Faggs Manor. Mr. Blair was eminently distinguished for his talents, piety and usefulness in the Church, and was esteemed one of the most able, learned, and excellent men of his day. He established a classical school at Faggs Manor, which had particular reference to the study of theology, and from which eminated many distinguished pupils, who did honor to their instructor, both as scholars and Christian ministers, among whom may be mentioned the Rev. Samuel Davies, called in his day "the prince of preachers," and who was one of the presidents of the College of New Jersey; the Rev. John Rodgers, for a long time an eminent minister in New York; and Rev. Robert Smith, of Pequea, the father of Samuel Stanhope Smith and John Blair Smith, all eminent as scholars and divines.

Mr. Blair's daughters married respectively Rev. George Duffield, Rev. David Rice, of Kentucky, Rev. John Carmichael, of Forks of Brandywine, Rev. William Foster, of Upper Octorara, Dr. Samuel Edmiston, a physician of Faggs Manor, Mr. James Moore, a farmer, and a Mr. Sanderson, a merchant. I may be permitted to refer to Mr. Carmichael, as a man who possessed a mind of more than ordinary comprehensiveness and energy, and as an eloquent, laborious and faithful minister. In the Revolution, he was an earnest and uncompromising friend of American liberty, and did much to animate the drooping spirit of the people, during the whole of that contest. He succeeded in instilling the principles of patriotism into the minds of the people to whom he ministered to such an extent that when they were called upon to serve their country, not a man capable of bearing arms hesitated or faltered, and, in their absence, it devolved upon the old men, women and children to attend to the ordinary farm work. Mr. Carmichael's will, which is on record in the register's office of Chester county, contains a synopsis of the doctrines and polity of the Presbyterian Church, as given in her standards, and an expression of his belief in them. It is a curious document.

Mr. Foster was succeeded as pastor of the united congregations of Upper Octorara and Doe Run by Rev. Alexander Mitchel, who was installed at Octorara December 14, 1785, giving Doe Run one-fourth of his time. The congregation had in the meantime received supplies from Presbytery, those most frequently appointed being the Rev. Robert Smith, of Pequea, and Rev. John Carmichael, of Forks of Brandywine.

Mr. Mitchel was born in 1731, graduated at the College of New Jersey in 1765, was licensed in April, 1767, and ordained in November, 1768. Previous to coming to Octorara and Doe Run, he had been pastor of the church of Deep Run, in Bucks county. He was fifty-four years of age, and had been eighteen years in the ministry when he became pastor of this church.

He purchased from Colonel Andrew Boyd one hundred and fifty acres of the farm formerly of Rev. Adam Boyd, including the buildings, and removed there in the spring of 1786. Colonel Boyd then removed to that part of the property now known as the Armstrong farm, where he resided until his death.

Towards the close of Mr. Foster's pastorate, an improvement was made in the music of the sanctuary. Rouse's version of the Psalms was then in use, and the precentor confined himself to a very few well known tunes, so that there was not much variety in the singing. The young folks, however, had begun to visit Philadelphia, and had picked up ideas in advance of their seniors, and in course of time, through their influence, the old precentor or clerk, who led the singing, was placed upon the retired list, and a new and younger one installed, with the view of introducing new tunes. These intended innovations upon the established order of things of course occasioned considerable discussion. As a general rule, the older members preferred the few tunes they had been accustomed to from childhood, and which, with them, were surrounded with an air of sanctity; while the junior members, who had no particular reverence for the "good old ways," upheld the new measures. On the first Sabbath that the new state of affairs was inaugurated, when the precentor rose to lead the singing, and opened with a new tune, Elder James Glendenning, who sat in the elders' pew in front of the pulpit, arose, and, with mournful visage and slow and solemn step, walked out of the house. That tune was known for some time thereafter among the young folks as "Glendenning's March."

Soon after Mr. Mitchel became pastor, the congregation took another step in advance, by introducing

UPPER OCTORARA GRAVEYARD AND OLD SESSION HOUSE.

Watts' Psalms and Hymns in place of Rouse's version of the Psalms, which up to this period had been in use. In this, the congregation were quite in advance of other Presbyterian churches, as generally Rouse's version continued to be used until a much later period.

In 1790, the wall of the graveyard, which had become dilapidated, was rebuilt. The yard was at the same time enlarged on the north side by rebuilding the wall about twenty feet further to the north. You can see at the present day where the old wall stood on that side. The trustees of the church who had charge of this rebuilding, were Samuel McClellan, Arthur Park, Thomas Heslip, Joseph Park, and Joseph Gardner. The mason work was done by Robert McClellan, a son of Samuel McClellan, one of the trustees. The ground thus enclosed was about fifty-seven yards in front by seventy-one yards deep, and contained about one hundred and thirty-five square perches, and remained of this size until it was again enlarged after the erection of the present church building. On one of the upright stones at the side of the entrance, Mr. McClellan, the mason, carved the initials of his name, "R. McC.," and underneath them the date, "1790." That stone forms one of the sides of the present gateway, and bears the initials and date I have mentioned.

We obtain a knowledge of the principal families that formed the congregation at this period, from the list of the subscribers to the building of this wall, which contains about sixty names. The amount subscribed was £35, besides a considerable amount in labor and use of teams.*

About the same period, stoves were for the first time introduced into the church. Before this was done, the people had no means of warming themselves except in the session-house, which, being small, many of them entered the cold church and sat through two services, and returned home, without going near the fire. When the building was erected, no provision had been made for warming it, and when the stoves were placed in it, a hole was cut through the centre of the roof, and the pipes from the stoves connected overhead, and carrried up through it.

It may strike you as somewhat singular that our forefathers should make no provision for warming the houses of worship erected by them. It must be remembered, however, that stoves are an institution of comparatively modern invention, and that in the olden time there was no convenient way of heating large spaces. For some time after the first introduction of stoves, people looked with distrust on the new contrivances for warming their houses, preferring the large open fire-places to which they were accustomed.

In the year 1795, difficulties arose in the congregation, at first a mere speck on the horizon, which soon increased to such an extent that its very existence was for a time threatened, and from the effects of which it did not recover for many years.

A ball was held at a new public house within the

* See Appendix E.

bounds of the congregation, which was attended by many of the young people. On the first Sabbath thereafter, Mr. Mitchel took occasion to preach against the propriety of members of the church attending and engaging in such festivities, and in doing so, indulged in very strong language, and denounced those who had engaged in it with much vehemence. As one of my informants forcibly expressed it, "he gave them a regular tearing up about it."

The people became intensely excited, some sustaining Mr. Mitchel, and others inveighing against him, not so much on account of his opposition to the ball, as to the manner in which he alluded to those who had attended it. Matters came to such a pitch, that one Sabbath the church was locked against Mr. Mitchel, and the Bible taken away. He procured one of his servants, a colored man named James Howell, to enter the house through the small window which lighted the pulpit, and which he reached by means of a ladder. In this way the house was opened, and the services conducted as usual; Mr. Mitchel making use of a small Bible which he carried with him.

It is related of James Howell, who was a man of considerable intelligence for one in his position, that when he was about entering through the window, he said to Mr. Mitchel, "This is not right." Upon Mr. Mitchel inquiring the reason, he replied, "Because the good book says, 'He that entereth not by the door into the sheep-fold, but climbeth up some other way, the same is a thief and a robber.'"

The opposition to Mr. Mitchel still continuing, he,

on the 6th of January, 1796, requested Presbytery to dissolve the pastoral relation, as expressed in the minutes of Presbytery, " in consequence of some unhappy differences subsisting between him and some members of his congregation." The Presbytery declined to grant the request, and appointed a committee to visit the congregation, and inquire into the state of matters, with a view, if possible, of healing the differences. At the next meeting of Presbytery, held May 5, 1796, this committee reported that there appeared to be considerable differences among the people, which they were unable to heal, and referred the matter to Presbytery. Mr. Mitchel renewed his request, that the pastoral relation might be dissolved; and, after hearing Mr. Mitchel and commissioners from the congregation, the Presbytery acquiesced in the propriety of the request, " both for the peace and harmony of the congregation, as well as the usefulness and comfort of Mr. Mitchel," and the pastoral relation was accordingly dissolved.

These difficulties did not extend to the congregation of Doe Run, which was harmonious and peaceable, and over which Mr. Mitchel continued to exercise a fatherly care until the year 1809, when, by reason of advancing years, he was unable longer to minister to them.

At the next meeting of Presbytery, after the pastoral relation of Mr. Mitchel was dissolved, John Fleming and Arthur Park appeared as elders and representatives from this congregation, and requested that Mr. Mitchel should be appointed to supply the pulpit for six months, he engaging to visit ministerially every family within the bounds of the congregation, and if possible remove all difficulties; Mr. Fleming and Mr. Park engaging, so far as their influence extended, to encourage and strengthen his hands in the undertaking.

The request was granted, and Mr. Mitchel entered upon the very arduous undertaking of endeavoring to unite a divided congregation. As might be anticipated, he did not succeed, and so reported to Presbytery at its next meeting. The Presbytery deemed it best that the pastoral relation should remain dissolved, and enjoined it upon both him and the congregation, that they should studiously avoid every thing which might alienate their affections or be productive of discord.

In October, 1797, Mr. Mitchel and commissioners from the congregation were again before Presbytery, on the subject of his preaching within the bounds of the congregation; and the Presbytery enjoined it upon him that he should not officiate, unless he was called upon to do so, by appointment of Presbytery, or the unanimous request of the session, and admonished the congregation that they should be at peace among themselves, and endeavor to attain such a state of union and strength as would enable them to obtain the services of a regular pastor.

This injunction and admonition seem not to have been heeded, as in October, 1798, the Presbytery was informed that fresh causes of disaffection and discord had arisen, growing out of the conduct of Mr.

Mitchel, in baptizing the children of some of the members, and granting certificates of dismission to other churches. The Presbytery again enjoined it upon Mr. Mitchel not to perform any ministerial acts within the bounds of the congregation, unless invited by the session, or appointed thereto by the Presbytery, and also requested the session to cheerfully accept the services of Mr. Mitchel when not otherwise supplied. After this, we hear of no further difficulties between Mr. Mitchel and the congregation, except as to the payment of his salary, which was in arrears, and which was not finally settled until December, 1800, nearly five years after he ceased to be pastor.

In September, 1799, the Presbytery met at Upper Octorara, with the view of endeavoring to heal the dissensions in the congregation, and after a conference with the respective parties, happily succeeded in their object. The following paper was adopted and signed by seventy-one members of the church, including all the heads of families:

"We, the subscribers, members constituting the congregation of Upper Octorara, deeply impressed with the threatening aspect of being deprived of the stated means of grace amongst us, and humbled under a sense of our own neglect and departure from God, which have provoked the Divine Majesty of heaven to permit divisions and dissensions to take such place amongst us as to threaten the peace and unity of this branch of his church, to the wounding of the interest of religion in general, as well as our own souls:

And whereas, it hath been proposed by the malcontents that the election of eleven ruling elders, in which the present session shall be polled for in common with others, would remove their objections, and upon that condition they were willing to unite with their brethren, and heartily to join with them in adopting such rules and regulations as to a majority might appear to tend to the happiness, peace and good order of the congregation. And as the measure has been advised by the Presbytery, and with a view to remove every complaint, and heal the divisions subsisting, it hath been acceded to by the present session:

Therefore, we whose names are hereunto subscribed, do bind ourselves to each other to abide by and adhere to the following resolves:

I. *Resolved,* That subscribing this instrument and these resolves which shall be considered the enrollment of the members of this congregation, shall be the test of membership.

II. *Resolved,* That so soon as six ruling elders shall be chosen and ordained to their office, the present ruling elders, except those re-elected, shall cease to act any longer in that office.

III. *Resolved,* That we will submit to and abide by the decision of a majority of the Session, in all matters coming under their jurisdiction, and also to a majority of the regular members of this congregation, in any matter appertaining to the congregation, and in particular with respect to our obtaining the stated means of grace amongst us.

IV. *Resolved,* That any person, a member of this congregation, doing or countenancing any thing or measure which may appear to the Session to operate against the peace and unity of the congregation, such person or persons shall be dealt with and censured agreeably to the discipline of our church, and the true intent and meaning of these resolves.

V. *Resolved,* That any person wishing to withdraw from this society (which withdrawal shall be a request to the Session to have his name erased from this enrollment, and a certificate), shall offer his reasons to the Session, which, if by them deemed sufficient, he shall obtain a certificate agreeably to his standing, and that, before he is received by any other society, or otherwise, the session may refer him for a decision in the premises, to the Presbytery.

VI. *Resolved,* That during the vacancy of this congregation, a majority of the Session shall order and regulate applications for supplies.

Done at Upper Octorara, September 11, 1799.

Gideon Irwin,
John Fleming, Sen.,
Arthur Park,
Henry McClellan,
George Boyd,
Robert McClellan,
Thomas Heslep,
John Smith,
Thomas Hope,
John Park,
Richard McClure,
John Hershberger,
Adam Cowan,
James Cowan,
Thomas Scott,
John Scott,
Samuel Wilson,
Hannah Kinkead,
John Pinkerton,
John Fleming, Jr.,
George Richmond,
Samuel McClellan,
James Boyd,
John G. Parke,
John Fleming, of East Caln,
Francis Gardner,
James Boyd,
John Morrison,
George Sloan,
Joseph Sloan,
John Sloan,
Mary Glendenning,
Richard McPherson,

Alexander McPherson,
Thomas Hull,
Joseph Cowan,
Oliver Wells,
William Boyd,
David Gilfillan,
Paul Price,
William Stewart,
John Wallace,
James Scott,
James McClellan,
Adam Glendenning,
Widow Kirkpatrick,
William Davidson,
Andrew Stewart
Samuel Wright,
Wallace Boyd,
John Irwin,
Robert Young,
John Porter,
William Harper,
John McPherson,
Archibald Gilfillan,
Jenny Park,
Robert Hamilton,
Joseph Park,
Samuel Futhey,
George McWilliams,
Jane Boyd,
James Withrow,
Catharine Boyd,
Hannah Hope,
John Hamill,

Israel Hamill,   Henry Blott,
Elisha Hamill,   Samuel McClellan.
Isaac Wentz,

After the foregoing paper was adopted and signed, the congregation proceeded to the election of ruling elders, and re-elected the six old elders and also five new ones. Those re-elected, so far as I can obtain their names, were Gideon Irwin, John Fleming, Sen., Arthur Park, Henry McClellan, and George Boyd. The new ones elected were John Fleming. Jr., Thomas Hope, James Boyd. Adam Cowan, and James Cowan.

The five new elders were duly ordained, and peace and harmony, which had been interrupted for a period of four years, again reigned in Octorara.

The list of names appended to the paper I have just read is interesting, as furnishing us with the names of the heads of families of the congregation at the close of the last, and beginning of the present century. In this list of seventy-one names, there are forty surnames; and of these, about twenty-five are borne by members of the congregation at this time.

Early in the present century, the church was struck with lightning. which shattered the east door, and otherwise injured the building, rendering considerable repairs necessary.

No effort seems to have been made to elect a pastor until September 9, 1809, when calls were presented to Rev. Robert White to become pastor of Upper Octorara and Doe Run; giving to Octorara three-fourths, and to Doe Run one-fourth of his time.

These calls were signed, on behalf of Upper Octorara, by ruling elders Arthur Park, George Boyd, Henry McClellan, John Fleming, Jr., James Cowan, and John Fleming, Sr.; and on behalf of Doe Run, by ruling elders Hugh Jordan, John Mitchell, and William Gordon, and attested by Rev. A. Mitchel as presiding minister. The salary promised was five hundred dollars, of which three hundred and seventy-five was to be paid by Upper Octorara, and one hundred and twenty-five by Doe Run.

At the meeting of Presbytery, at which these united calls were placed in the hands of Mr. White, calls were also presented to him by the congregation of Faggs Manor, and also by the united congregations of White Clay Creek and Head of Christina. Of these three calls, he accepted that from Faggs Manor, and was ordained and installed there on December 14, 1809.

It is a singular coincidence, that in 1768, when Mr. Foster accepted the call from Upper Octorara and Doe Run, he had in his hands calls from the same churches that Mr. White had in 1809.

On the 24th of September, 1810, a call was extended by Upper Octorara to Rev. James Latta for three-fourths of his time, for which they agreed to pay him a salary of four hundred dollars. This call was signed by Rev. Robert White as Moderator of the Congregational Meeting, and by Arthur Park, George Boyd, Henry McClellan, and John Fleming, Jr., ruling elders.*

* See Appendix F.

Mr. Latta had been licensed by the Presbytery of New Castle, at New London, December 13, 1809, and had in the meantime preached to a congregation in West Chester county, New York. At the meeting of Presbytery, at which the call from Upper Octorara was placed in his hands, a letter was received from the congregation in West-Chester county, New York, requesting Presbytery to grant liberty to Mr. Latta to continue his labors there, with a view to their settling him as their pastor.

Mr. Latta declined the invitation from New York, accepted the call from Upper Octorara, and was, on the 2d of April, 1811, ordained and installed. In this service, the Rev. N. W. Sample presided; the Rev. John E. Latta preached the ordination sermon, and the Rev. Samuel Martin gave the charge to the pastor and people.

Mr. Latta's three elder brothers, Francis A. Latta, William Latta, and John E. Latta, all ministers, were present, and the ordination of their younger brother was doubtless to them an occasion of deep interest. They were desirous he should settle in Eastern Pennsylvania, and their wishes had probably much to do with his declining the invitation from New York, and accepting the call from Octorara.

When Mr. Latta was called to Octorara for three-fourths of his time, it was expected that Doe Run would extend a call to him for the remaining fourth. They declined to do so, and the connection between Upper Octorara and Doe Run, which had to some extent existed for seventy years, was thus severed, and from the year 1810 they have been distinct congregations.

As at this point we part company with the Doe Run Church, I will refer to such points in her history as I have not already spoken of.

The first Church edifice, a log structure, erected about 1740, stood within the grounds of the graveyard as at present enclosed. It was in this building George Whitefield preached during his visitation. In 1771, during the pastorate of Mr. Foster, the congregation erected their second edifice. It was of hewn logs, about nine hundred and sixty square feet in area, and stood between the present church and the graveyard. The present building was erected in 1821. It is of stone, and its dimensions are fifty-three by forty feet.

During the pastorate of Mr. Sterling, Captain John Montgomery became a ruling elder. Mr. Foster ordained to that office Andrew Mitchell, Robert Cowan, and John Wiley; and Mr. Mitchel ordained Hugh Jordan, Robert Morsel, William Hanna, and James Steen.

It would be interesting to relate the further history of that church, but it is foreign to our purpose, and would extend too much the limits of this discourse. I will briefly say, that Rev. Samuel Henderson was pastor about one year and a half in 1813 and 1814, when he removed to Williamsport; Rev. Elkanah Kelsay Dare from May 13, 1817, until his death, August 26, 1826; Rev. Alexander G. Morrison from April 24, 1828, to October 6, 1857; Rev. John

Wynne Martin, D.D., from April 13, 1858, to October 19, 1860; and Rev. John P. Clarke from June, 1865, to April, 1868. The pulpit is now vacant, and supplied by Presbytery.

Mr. Latta, for two years after his installation, preached the one-fourth of his time at the Gap, in Lancaster county, where a portion of the members of his congregation resided. On September 29, 1812, he received from Upper Octorara a call for his entire pastoral labors, at a salary of five hundred dollars, which he accepted, and this church, for the first time in her history, had the entire services of a pastor.

You will have seen, from the dates I have given you, that from May, 1796, to September, 1810, a period of fourteen years and four months, this congregation was without a pastor. During this vacancy it received supplies from Presbytery.

As it may be interesting to know what ministers filled the pulpit during this long interval, I will give you their names, as I have culled them from the minutes of Presbytery, to wit: "Colin McFarquhar, N. W. Sample, Francis Hindman, David McConoughey, John B. Patterson, William Latta, Patrick Dawson, William Stewart, Nathan Grier, Joseph Barr, Alexander Mitchel, John E. Latta, Robert Kennedy, Dr. James Latta, William Arthur, Joshua Knight, Charles Cummings, James Magraw, Stewart Williamson, John Waugh, Thomas Hood, Francis A. Latta, John D. Perkins, Caleb Johnson, William Kerr, James Buchanan, Alexander Boyd, Nathaniel R. Snowden, Robert White, and John F. Grier.

One of these, Robert Kennedy, supplied the pulpit for several months, with a view to his being settled as pastor, but the congregation were unable to unite upon him. He was a brother of Maxwell Kennedy, of the Rising Sun, near the Gap, in Lancaster county, who was well known to many of the older persons in this audience.

The most popular of these supplies were the Rev. Nathan Grier, of Brandywine Manor, Rev. William Arthur, of Pequea, and Rev. Nathaniel W. Sample, of Leacock. Whenever it was known they were to preach, crowds usually attended the services. People would walk for miles to attend upon their ministry. Mr. Grier had a strong, full and melodious voice, and when preaching in the open air, could be heard for a considerable distance. If the weather was warm, he did not scruple to take off his coat while preaching When there was no preacher, Elder Arthur Park sometimes led the services, and read a printed sermon.

After the adjustment, in 1799, of the difficulties in the congregation, Mr. Mitchel was an occasional supply, both by appointment of Presbytery and by invitation from the Session. He had many warm friends in the congregation, and was held in much estimation.

In person, he was tall and spare, and of venerable aspect; was very social in his disposition, kind and affectionate, instructive in conversation, and a pleasant, companionable man. As a preacher, however, he was not popular. He was a scholar, and a man of excellent mind, but very slow and tedious in his delivery, especially in his later years.

Like all the large landed proprietors of that day, he was the owner of slaves. One of them, James Howell, already referred to, was quite intelligent, and a great favorite.

About the year 1809 or 1810, Mr. Mitchel, having become advanced in years, and having no children, accepted an invitation to spend the remainder of his days in the family of Robert Cochran, near the village of Cochranville. He was remotely connected with Mr. Cochran, and had been a frequent visitor at his house. Here he resided about three years, and died on the 6th of December, 1812, at the age of eighty-one years. His remains rest in yonder churchyard, covered with a tasteful monument, on which is carved an appropriate tribute to his memory.

In 1812, a few months prior to his death, he sold his farm, which he had purchased from Colonel Andrew Boyd, in 1786, to Rev. James Latta.

When Mr. Latta first came to Octorara, he boarded with James Boyd, who lived near the church; afterwards he resided for some years in the family of Thomas McClellan. He was married on the 15th of October, 1815, and for about six months resided in the house of the late Robert Futhey, then recently erected, in (now) Highland township. In the Spring of 1816, he removed to the farm he had purchased from Mr. Mitchel in 1812.

With the installation of Mr. Latta, the congregation took, as it were, a new lease of life, and set out on its journey with renewed vigor. He was young and energetic, of popular manners, and earnest in the Master's cause, and imparted to those with whom he was brought in contact a portion of his own vitality.

The long vacancy had so reduced their numbers that when he became pastor, the membership did not much exceed one hundred.

In 1813, the Session commenced to keep a regular registry of admissions to the church, and of baptisms and deaths. There were then on the roll one hundred and forty-seven members. Additions were made to it at every communion season, and the congregation soon became strong and vigorous.

The early Scotch and Irish Presbyterian emigrants brought with them the customs and modes of worship of the churches at home. One of these was that of having two consecutive services on the Sabbath, with an intermission of half an hour. This custom prevailed in this congregation from the earliest times until about the year 1812. The people, during the interval between the services, were accustomed to visit the spring on the opposite side of the road from the present residence of Oliver P. Wilson, for the purpose of allaying their thirst. I cannot better describe the scene during the intermission than in the words of a poem published a few years since, a portion of which I beg leave to quote:

> "Blest sight it was, to mark that godly flock,
>   At intermission, grouped throughout this wood,
> Each log, each bench, each family upping block,
>   Some grand-dame held amidst her gathered brood;

    Here cakes were shared, and fruits. and counsel good.
        Devoutly spoken 'twas of crops and rain ;
    Hard by the church the broad-brimmed elders stood.
        While o'er that slope did flow a constant train
    Of bevies, springward bound, or coming back again.

"Ah! luckless wight, whom gallantry did press
    Fast by that spring, to stoop him often low,
And serve, with cup up-dipped, and bland address,
    The gathered fair, whose multitude did grow !
One whom he most affects, and did bestow
    Her first the cup, hath drunk, and off does walk ;
Her then to follow fain he must forego,—
    With some far happier swain he marks her talk.
While he must stoop, and grin, and water all the flock.

"Here too, like me, some lonesome wight of yore
    Did stand apart, and these memorials scan,
And blighted hopes and buried loves deplore,
    And feel, in sooth, how frail a thing is man.
Hither the widow came, weeping and wan,
    To muse on him of late her joy and pride.
Ah! now no more she mourns the solemn ban
    Which did her then from her loved spouse divide—
Now does she sleep herself all sweetly by his side."*

The morning service was generally of considerable length—that in the afternoon not so long; but the entire services occupied the greater portion of the day, and night was generally drawing on apace when the people reached their homes. It was to them a matter-of-course, and they thought of nothing else but spending the day at church, and were not satisfied unless the sermons were of considerable length.

    * See Nevin's Churches of the Valley, p. 45.

They desired good measure, full and running over. What a change has taken place in this respect. *Then*, the preacher did not confine himself within the period of an hour in the delivery of his discourse, but frequently exceeded that limit. *Now*, the pews become very uneasy if the sermon exceeds half an hour in length, and are in tortures if it reaches fifty minutes.

Mr. Latta, soon after the commencement of his pastorate, abolished this practice of having two services in the church on Sabbath, deeming it better that the afternoon services should be held at private houses or school-houses at different points within the bounds of the congregation. This change was not made without creating considerable dissatisfaction. The people were wedded to their old customs, and did not readily acquiesce in the new order of things. Some of our good grandmothers, it has been related to me, were very indignant at being sent home from church in the middle of the day.

Mr. Latta, about the same time, gave the death blow to another custom which had been brought from the fatherland; that of furnishing intoxicating drinks at funerals. The custom was, when the people were assembled at the funeral house, as it was termed, to carry around cakes and liquors, of which all, young and old, generally partook. Sometimes some thirsty soul would take his position where he would be served among the first, and then would be found on the outskirts, where those serving were about concluding their round. Mr. Latta saw the evil of this custom, and gradually prevailed upon the people to abandon it.

In this connection, I may mention that the earliest form of hearse in use in this congregation was on two wheels. Sloats or pieces were nailed across the shafts, and the coffin was placed on them and strapped. The undertaker rode on horseback and led the horse attached to the hearse. Adam Glendenning was for a long time an undertaker, and used this form of vehicle.

John Hershberger, who succeeded Adam Glendenning as an undertaker, introduced a four-wheeled hearse, the body of it shaped like a coffin. This was used for many years, and until the modern open vehicle came into use.

In early times, the people performed their journeys either on foot or on horseback. Riding carriages were not in use, and the two-wheeled hearse would be the only vehicle at a funeral. Upping blocks were of course very numerous in the church grounds.

The first riding vehicle in the congregation was a "chair" belonging to the Rev. Mr. Mitchel. The first four-wheeled carriage was introduced by Elder John Fleming, Sr.; the second, a large one, capable of holding six persons, by Samuel McClellan; and the third, about 1814, by Elder Arthur Park. After this, they became more common, although for many years thereafter, people very generally rode on horseback, the same horse frequently performing the task of carrying two persons at one time; sometimes the wife on a pillion behind her husband, sometimes a child.

When it was likely to rain, the people would take the saddles from their horses, and place them in the session-house, or underneath the church. If it commenced to rain during the services, the men would go out for the same purpose, and the pastor would sometimes suspend the exercises while this was being done.

Parasols in those days were unknown, the women carrying large fans to shield their faces from the rays of the sun. Umbrellas were used to a limited extent.

This church was incorporated on the 6th of May, 1812. The first board of trustees* named in the charter were Francis Gardner, John Fleming, of East Caln, Wallace Boyd, Joseph Richmond, Samuel Boyd, Thomas Scott, and James Boyd, who held their first meeting at the house of Wallace Boyd, on the 4th of July, 1812, and organized by appointing Francis Gardner as President, Wallace Boyd as Treasurer, and Joseph Richmond as Secretary.

Sunday-schools were established in the congregation about the year 1818. They were first organized at the session house, and at the school-house near the present residence of Ezekiel R. Young. Soon afterwards they were organized at Hollis' School-house, now the tenant house on the farm late of William Stewart, in Highland township, at the school-house known as "The Pass," and at other points. Mrs.

* See Appendix G. and H.

Latta was very active in promoting the establishment of these schools.

In 1822 and 1823, an extensive revival of religion took place in the congregation. It was greatly promoted by a female prayer meeting, usually held at the house of Mrs. Mary McClellan—Aunt Polly McClellan, as she was generally called. She resided on the farm lately occupied by her grandson, Samuel Parke McClellan, deceased. As the fruits of this revival, seventy-nine persons were admitted to church privileges in the year 1822, and forty-five persons in 1823.

In the year 1824, the interior arrangements of the church were entirely altered. The pulpit, a new one, was placed in the east end, two aisles ran the length of the room from east to west, there was a space across the church in front of the pulpit, an aisle across the west end, and a short aisle from the south door to the nearest east and west aisle. There were four ranges of pews; a double range in the middle, and single ranges against the north and south walls, and also on each side of the pulpit. The pulpit was elaborately ornamented, and was reached by winding stairs at the north side. It was open underneath. In front of it was a railing, behind which the precentors stood while leading the singing. The pew doors were painted white, and the numbers painted on them in large black figures.

The church, after these alterations, was at first heated by two stoves, placed at the north and south sides; afterwards two more were added, one of them placed in the space in front of the pulpit, and the other in the aisle at the west end.

A trap door was placed in this west aisle, which was afterwards put to a use perhaps not contemplated when it was made.

In those days it was customary for the dogs to accompany their masters to church, and they frequently came into the building, and perambulated the aisles, to the disturbance of the worshipers. Thomas Ross, the sexton, conceived the idea of putting a stop to this annoyance, and accordingly, placing himself by this trap and watching his opportunity, divers of the canine species were arrested in their course, and transferred to the space underneath the floor, there to remain in durance until the congregation were dismissed, when they were released by the outer door. This novel expedient proved successful, and the canines were generally thereafter among the stay-at-homes.

More than one urchin was put upon his good behavior, by being admonished that unless he was a good boy in meeting, Tommy Ross would put him in the dog-hole; and there are those present to-day who will perhaps remember having received such an admonition.

While the alterations were being made, Mr. Latta desired to have a bell placed upon the church. Some of the people were accustomed to sit on the upping blocks and on the graveyard wall, until they heard Mr. Latta's voice giving out the opening psalm. Mr. Latta gave as a reason for having a bell, that he did not wish to have to make use of the Psalms of David to call the people into the church. The trustees, however, seem to have considered a bell a superfluity, as none was erected.

The system of renting the pews first came into use at this time. The salary of the pastor had theretofore been collected by stipends, each person being assessed what was esteemed his proportion.

Before the alteration, the communion was wholly administered at tables placed in the long aisle in front of the pulpit. Afterwards, there being less room in front of the pulpit. some of the front pews were used for that purpose, in addition to tables. In accordance with the Scottish custom, leaden tokens were used on these occasions. They were given out by the pastor and elders to those entitled to partake of the sacrament, and taken up after they were seated at the tables. These tokens were flat pieces of lead something over half an inch square, with the letters "U. O.," the initials of the name of the church, stamped upon them. I have some of them in my possession. The use of these tokens was abolished when the alterations of which I have just spoken were made in the church.

The old Scottish custom of "fencing the tables," as it was called, *i. e.* prohibiting the approach of those who were deemed unworthy to receive the communion, was practiced until about the same time. This ceremony usually consisted of the delivery of a short address by the minister to the intending communicants, upon the sacredness of the rite, debarring the ignorant and profane from approaching the table, and stating the characteristics of worthy communicants.

The communion service consisted of two large, and four small mugs of pewter. These continued to be used until the congregation entered the present building in 1840, when a silver service was presented to the church. What became of the pewter service I do not know. It should have been sacredly preserved.

It was customary in former times to have services on the Thursday preceding the communion. This day was known as the preparation or fast day, and was very generally observed. These communion occasions generally drew together large crowds of persons from a considerable distance.

The first mode of taking up collections in the church, was with small square boxes placed on the end of poles, with the top of the box half covered. Afterwards the trustees took their stand at the church doors after service, with their hats in their hands, and the people as they passed out dropped their contributions in the hats. When the church was altered in 1824, velvet bags with long handles attached were introduced, and used until about the year 1866, when they gave way to the present basket system.

The custom of lining the psalm, as it was termed, which was practiced under the earlier pastors, was discontinued in the ordinary services, soon after Mr. Latta became pastor; the people, at his suggestion, generally supplying themselves with Watts' Psalms and Hymns.

On communion occasions however, the hymns which were sung while the people were coming forward to the tables, were lined by the elders, and this practice continued until the congregation entered the present building in 1840.

It was formerly also very customary in singing, to repeat the last two lines of the last verse. This, however, was not always done, and occasionally some member of the congregation who was dull of hearing, not observing that the clerks had taken their seats, would repeat the last lines by himself, somewhat to the amusement of the young folks, and perhaps of some of the seniors.

Another custom to which I will advert, was that of announcing evening services during a portion of the year, "to commence at early candle-light." This was very common in my young days, but I believe has now fallen into disuse.

About the year 1828, societies for the suppression of the vice of intemperance were formed. Mr. Latta, from the initiatory movement, was an ardent friend and advocate of the cause, and during the whole course of his ministry, did all in his power for its advancement. In the minutes of the Presbytery of New Castle, under the date of April 1, 1828, I find this entry written on the margin of the record of the proceedings of the meeting, held that day at the Church of Lower Brandywine: "Presbytery entertained without ardent spirits for the first time—tea substituted." It is in the bold handwriting of Rev. E. W. Gilbert, the then clerk of Presbytery. The

Church of Lower Brandywine is therefore entitled to the honor of breaking up an old, but baleful custom. The Presbytery, at this same meeting, took strong and decided ground in favor of the temperance movement.

In 1831, what were then known as "four days meetings," and afterwards as protracted meetings, are first mentioned in the minutes of Presbytery. The Presbytery recommended that "twilight prayer-meetings," should be held for special prayer for a revival of religion, and the members were divided into classes, for the purpose of holding "four days meetings" in their respective congregations. Meetings of this kind, commencing on Tuesday and ending on Friday, were held in this church in the years 1831, 1832 and 1833, which were very largely attended, and resulted in an ingathering in 1831, of thirty-nine members; in 1832, of fifty-three members; and in 1833, of forty-two members.

In 1832, the bounds of the congregation were curtailed, by the organization of a church at Belleview, and in 1833 by the organization at Coatesville.

About the year 1836, through the exertions of Mr. Latta, a church building was erected in Sadsburyville, as a place of preaching in the afternoon and evening, and for the use of the Sunday-school, which has been very serviceable to the portion of the congregation residing in that vicinity. This property was conveyed by Martin Armstrong to the trustees of this church, by deed dated January 31, 1844. A deed had been previously made, which was lost. The school directors of Sadsbury, have an interest in the basement room, in which, for many years one of the public schools of the township was held.

In 1839, the church edifice in which this congregation worshiped, having become dilapidated and being deemed unsafe, the sense of the congregation was taken on the subject of repairing the old house, or erecting a new one. After deliberation—although there was some diversity of sentiment on the subject—it was deemed best to erect a new building, and subscriptions were accordingly made for that purpose. On the 4th of March, 1840, Martin Armstrong, Robert Futhey and Samuel D. McClellan, were appointed a building committee, to whom the charge of the whole work was committed. The new building—the one in which we are now assembled, and the fourth church edifice on these grounds—was erected in the summer of 1840. It was dedicated on the 16th day of December of that year, the Rev. Alfred Nevin preaching in the morning, and Rev. William Latta, brother of the pastor, preaching the dedicatory sermon in the afternoon. The old edifice was torn down in May, 1840, and a part of the materials used in the construction of the new one. The cost of the new building when fully completed, was about forty-one hundred dollars, in addition to the value of the materials procured from the old one. Its outside size is fifty-seven and a half, by seventy feet; the audience room, exclusive of the gallery, is fifty-seven by fifty-four feet, and the height of the ceiling is twenty-one and a half feet. The number of pews on the ground floor is 104. The gallery is thirteen feet wide, and extends across the south end of the building, and will seat about 100 persons. The pulpit erected when the church was built, was quite wide. It was taken away in 1866, and the present one constructed.

When the old church was torn away, the graveyard was enlarged, by extending it twenty yards on the west side, and taking in the greater part of the ground where the old building had stood; and also taking in a space fourteen yards wide, on the south side; making its present size, ninety yards from east to west, and seventy-one yards from north to south, and its contents about one acre and a third.

The site of the old building has been recently marked by four stones put up at the corners, so that it may be known in the future where it stood.

Of the committee who had charge of the erection of this building, two have gone to their reward; the third, I am happy to see, is present with us to-day.

In 1840, when the congregation commenced to worship in this edifice, the roll of the church contained the names of two hundred and forty-five persons, who were in full communion.

With the demolition of the old church building, that time-honored race of officers in this church, known as precentors, also passed away. Those of you whose recollections extend back of the thirty years which have run their course since then, will recall the voices of Arthur Parke, Thomas Scott, Captain Thomas Stewart, Samuel W. Scott, James Fearon, William Whiteside, and others, as they led the congregation in the service of song. Methinks I yet see the venerable form, and hear the sonorous voice of Thomas Scott, as on communion occasions he lined the hymns, pronouncing the words, as was his wont, in one continuous tone. But those days have passed away, and live only in memory. The recollection of them, however, to me, and I doubt not to very many in this congregation, is sweet.

On the day this building was dedicated, the singing was for the first time led by a choir, which had been organized by Mr. Samuel W. Scott, and who continued to be its leader for eight years.

In former days, the services of this church were always opened with the singing of a psalm. The invocation was first used at the dedication of this building, in December, 1840.

The year 1849 witnessed a large addition to the membership, the result of a revival of religion with which the church was blessed in that year. In the religious services attending the work, Mr. Latta was greatly aided by the labors of Rev. John F. Cowan, who spent some time with the congregation.

Mr. Latta's connection with the church as pastor continued until October 1, 1850, when at his own request, the pastoral relation was dissolved. He had had it in contemplation for some time, to make this application at the end of a forty years' pastorate, and the day on which his relations to the church ceased, was precisely forty years from the day on which he took the oversight of it.

From the year 1813, when the Session commenced

to keep a roll of the membership of the church, until the termination of Mr. Latta's pastorate, there were added to the church, on examination and profession of their faith, five hundred and seventy-two, and on certificates from other churches, one hundred and twelve, making an average each year of fifteen on examination and three on certificate. During the same period, the ordinance of baptism was administered to six hundred and thirty-three infants, and one hundred and fifty-two adults.

Mr. Latta then engaged in missionary labor in Penningtonville and its neighborhood; and was instrumental in gathering a congregation and having a church edifice erected in that village, over which he was installed as pastor on the 11th of November, 1852. He maintained that relation until April 9, 1861, when, on account of increasing years, and the distance of his field of labor from his residence, the pastoral relation, at his request, was dissolved.

While he was pastor at Penningtonville, he procured, by his efforts, the erection of a church edifice at Christiana, about two miles from Penningtonville, to which he also ministered.

He died May 30, 1862, at the house of his nephew in Philadelphia, in which city he was attending the Pennsylvania Sabbath-School Convention, then in session. He was seated at the breakfast table, in apparent good health, when instantly life departed.

Mr. Latta was born at Chestnut Level, Pa., on the 10th of June, 1787. He was the youngest son of the Rev. James and Mary (McCalla) Latta. His father came from Ireland when he was about seven years of age, studied at the Synodical school at New London, in this county, graduated at the Philadelphia College, and studied theology under the Rev. Francis Alison, to whom he was related. He was pastor first at Deep Run, in Bucks county, and afterwards at Chestnut Level, where he died in 1801. He was the author of an excellent and exhaustive work on the subject of psalmody, published a few years before his death, designed to show that it is the duty of Christians to take the principal subjects and occasions of their psalms, hymns, and spiritual songs, from the gospel of Christ. He had four sons, Francis, William, John Ewing, and James, (all of whom became Presbyterian ministers,) and one son-in-law, the Rev. Thomas Love. The Rev. Robert P. Du Bois of New London, married a grand-daughter—the daughter of Rev. John E. Latta.

The Rev. James Latta was a man of remarkable energy and firmness in every good cause, and discharged with ability, high fidelity and unceasing earnestness, the duties of the Christian ministry over fifty-two years. He was indefatigable in ministerial labor, and preached a great deal at private houses and school-houses through the large bounds of his congregation. His style of preaching was earnest, animated, and impressive, and the matter of his sermons was solid and thoroughly evangelical.

He was a man of great readiness of speech, shrewd in silencing errorists, was quick-witted, ready at retort, and sometimes keenly satirical. He was an adversary that it was not always safe to attack in wordy war.

As an instance of his ready wit, I remember being present in the General Assembly in Philadelphia in 1861, of which he was a member, when some one was making a tedious speech. Mr. Latta called him to order; but being overruled by the Moderator, he remarked, in an under tone, that "it would be greatly to the consolation of the Assembly to have a few chapters of the book of Job read!"

As a pastor he was faithful, attentive to the young, the sick and afflicted, and very earnest in hunting up wanderers, and persuading people to attend upon the means of grace. He loved good singing, and excelled in it himself, and was a warm friend of Sabbath-schools.

This community in which he had his home, bears upon every hand the clear and deep traces of his life and character. None that ever crossed his threshhold can forget his cordial welcome, his graceful hospitality, or his genuine kindness, and there will long linger pleasant memories of his warm and abiding friendship, and his ministries of sympathy. He was extensively known, and so highly esteemed as a faithful Christian minister, that he became the centre of a very extended circle of acquaintanceship.

From my earliest recollection of him until he passed beyond mortal ken, I enjoyed his unbroken friendship, and I am glad to have this opportunity of paying my humble tribute to his memory.

On a most lovely day in the month of June, his

remains were borne to their resting place in yonder "city of the dead." His funeral was attended by a vast concourse of people from the surrounding country, and by many who gathered from distant parts. A very large number of his brethern in the ministry were also present to testify their high regard for his memory.

The monument in front of the family vault, is situated on the spot occupied by the pulpit of the old church, in which for thirty years he preached the everlasting gospel. He was the fourth pastor of this church, whose sepulchres are with us to this day, and whose united ministries within its walls extended over a period of more than a century.

The house in which Mr. Latta resided, had at the time of his death, been the residence of ministers of the gospel for about one hundred and twenty years.

During his ministerial life of fifty-two years, he performed the marriage ceremony three hundred and twenty-one times—the greatest number in any one year being in 1821, when he united seventeen couples.

The Rev. Francis A. Latta, the eldest brother of Rev. James Latta, was for some years a resident within the bounds of this congregation. He was ordained November 23, 1796, and was pastor successively of Presbyterian churches in Wilmington, Del., and Lancaster and Chestnut Level, Pa., in which latter place he also maintained a classical school for many years.

In the year 1826, he removed to Sadsbury township, Chester county, and established the "Moscow Academy," a classical and literary institution, which flourished for many years. I received my early classical education at this school, and have a very kindly remembrance of my preceptor. Of the teachers, I have gathered the names of Andrew Dinsmore, John McCullough, David McCarter, John M. Bear, John Turbitt, Gaylord L. More, and J. Smith Futhey. There were others, whose names I cannot recall. Of those I have mentioned, Mr. McCullough, Mr. McCarter, Mr. Bear, and Mr. More became ministers of the gospel. Robert Love, a brother of Rev. Thomas Love, who was a student for some years in this academy, also entered the ministry.

The Rev. Francis A. Latta was a man of remarkably well cultivated mind, a poet of no mean order, a very superior classical and Hebrew scholar, and one of the greatest instructors of the day. He was able in debate, clear, discriminating and decided in judgment, and a model in the pulpit. In his manners he was social, and in his deportment humble and unostentatious. He died April 21, 1834, at the age of sixty-seven, and was interred in the Upper Octorara burial ground.

As an historical item worth preserving in connection with the academy established by Mr. Latta, it may be mentioned, that about the close of the late war with Great Britain, there seems to have been a mania for laying out towns. John Pettit, who was the owner of a valuable tavern house and fifty acres of land in Sadsbury township, Chester county, on the

Lancaster and Philadelphia turnpike road, known as "The General Wayne," sold it, in the year 1814, to Abraham Brenneman and others, for the sum of *sixteen thousand dollars*. They laid out thereon *a town*, to which they gave the name of Moscow, from the city of Moscow, in Russia, then recently reduced by the flame, to prevent its occupation by the invading army of Napoleon Bonaparte. They undertook to dispose of the property by a lottery—the public house being the highest prize. Various lots were disposed of in this way, at prices ranging from two hundred and fifty to five hundred dollars, calling for streets bearing such Russian names as Cossacks, Wyburg, Alexander, Charlesburg, and others. One lot was set apart for a church, and another for a seminary. Fifteen lots, including the tavern house, which had been drawn by parties in Lancaster county, and containing altogether about four acres, were subsequently sold to Daniel Hiester and John Duer for eight thousand dollars.

The plot was gotten up in fine style, and presented an attractive appearance, but the *town* flourished only on paper. The project failed, and the lots, which had been purchased for eight thousand dollars, and on which a prudent money-lender had invested three thousand dollars on mortgage, were sold by the sheriff for thirteen hundred dollars. Cossacks street became again the common turnpike road, and the others returned to the bosom of the farm from which they had sprung.

It was on this property the "Moscow Academy"

was subsequently located, and from which it derived its name. It is now owned by George Lincoln.

In 1830, Rev. James Latta established a boarding school for girls called "The Mantua Female Seminary," which was for several years quite successful. At one time it had as many as thirty boarders, besides a number of day scholars. It occupied the building on the Lancaster and Philadelphia turnpike, now the residence of Dr. William S. Latta. Among the teachers were Miss Margaret McCullough, Miss Mary D. R. McCorkle, now Mrs. Mary D. R. Boyd, Miss Martha Wells and Miss Eliza Martin, now the wife of Rev. Gaylord L. More.

On the 26th of March, 1851, the Rev. James M. Crowell was elected pastor of the church, as the successor of Mr. Latta, and was ordained and installed by the Presbytery of New Castle on the 3d of June following. On this occasion, the Rev. Alfred Hamilton presided, Rev. John M. Dickey preached the ordination sermon, Rev. S. R. Wyncoop delivered the charge to the pastor, and Rev. A. G. Morrison the charge to the people. Mr. Crowell had been licensed by the Presbytery of Philadelphia on the 6th of January, 1851, while a student in the theological seminary at Princeton.

He was pastor until the 14th of April, 1857, when he was released to accept a call from the Seventh Presbyterian Church of Philadelphia, over which he was installed on the 10th of May of that year.

When he came to Octorara, the number of members was two hundred and forty-six. There were added during his pastorate, on profession of faith, ninety-seven, and on certificate forty-seven; and during the same period fifty-four infants and thirty-six adults were baptized. On the last occasion, on which he administered the communion, thirty-two were added to the church, as the fruits of a precious season of refreshing. At the close of his ministry here, the church numbered about three hundred and thirty members.

Mr. Crowell was born in Philadelphia, June 9, 1827. His father, Elisha Crowell, was for about thirty years a druggist and apothecary in that city. His mother, Susan McMullin, was the daughter of Robert McMullin, a ruling elder in the Pine Street or Third Presbyterian Church, during the pastorate of Dr. Archibald Alexander.

Mr. Crowell's preparation for college was made at the West Chester Academy, under the charge of Mr. James Crowell. He entered the sophomore class in the College of New Jersey, and graduated in 1848, about fourth in a class of eighty students. While in college, he was elected by his class-mates editor of the Nassau Literary Magazine, and by the American Whig Society was chosen one of four junior orators to represent the society in competition with four from the Cliosophic Society, at the centennial commencement of the college.

After his graduation, he taught the classics and mathematics at the West Chester Academy one year, and during that time pursued his theological studies under the direction of his cousin, Rev. John Crowell, preparatory to entering the seminary.

The degree of "Doctor of Divinity" was conferred upon him by Princeton College in December, 1864. He is now pastor of St. Peter's Church, Rochester, N. Y.

In a letter which I have recently received from Mr. Crowell, in speaking of his ministry among you, he says, "Never can I forget the clinging love, the tender constancy, the gentle kindness, the indulgent forbearance, the warm, welcoming cordiality, and the universal attachment of the dear people of Octorara Church. I lived among them nearly six years, and never once had my feelings wounded, nor my wishes crossed; and, when I left them, felt sure they all loved me. God bless them all!"

The Highland Presbyterian Church—an outpost of this congregation—was erected in the years 1851 to 1855, through the exertions of some ladies, who, by personal solicitation, secured the necessary funds, and was dedicated on the 14th day of June, 1855, the services being conducted by Mr. Crowell, assisted by Rev. Henry Steele Clarke, Rev. Robert P. Du Bois and Rev. Joseph E. Nassau.

It is used by the pastor of this church as a place of holding afternoon service, and during the summer by the Highland Sunday-school. A charter of incorporation was procured in 1851, the first board of trustees, consisting of Samuel Futhey, William Stewart and Israel McClellan. The present trustees are Israel McClellan, R. Agnew Futhey, and Jefferson Gibson.

Mr. Crowell was succeeded by Rev. Alexander

UPPER OCTORARA MANSE. ERECTED IN 1857.

Reed, a licentiate of the Presbytery of Washington, who was called on the 27th of June, 1857, and ordained and installed on the 8th of October following. The services were presided over by the Rev. James Otterson, who also gave the church to the pastor. The sermon was preached by the Rev. John Squier, and the charge to the people given by the Rev. Dr. Spottswood.

On the 10th of March, 1857, the congregation purchased from Joseph Stott one acre and a half of ground immediately adjoining the church property on the south, and in the summer of that year erected thereon a commodious and comfortable manse. The present fence around the church lot was constructed in 1859.

In 1862–3, during the war of the rebellion, Mr. Reed was in the service of the United States Christian Commission about six months as "general superintendent," and in that capacity—the duties of which were many and various, and performed with zeal and discretion—rendered very efficient service to the cause. He was also elected chaplain of the Second Pennsylvania Cavalry, but did not accept the position. During his absence, the pulpit was supplied by Mr. Frederick R. Wotring, then a licentiate of the Presbytery of Washington, now pastor of the Mansfield Church, in Allegheny county, Pa.

At a meeting of the Presbytery, held in this church in October, 1864, a call was presented to Mr. Reed from the Central Presbyterian Church of Philadelphia, which he held under consideration until the adjourned meeting of Presbytery during the sessions of Synod, when it was accepted by him, and his relation to this church was dissolved. His attachment to the people here was strong, and he severed the pastoral tie with very great reluctance, and only when advised by physicians that the preservation of his health required he should do so.

While Mr. Reed was pastor of this church, one hundred and eighty-six were added to its roll of membership on profession of faith, of whom eighty-one were added during the communion seasons of October, 1858, and April, 1859, the fruits of a revival of religion with which the church was blessed. During the same period, forty-one were added on certificate. The number of baptisms was seventy-six. At the communion season, in October, 1864, just previous to the close of his ministry here, thirty were added to the membership of the church.

Mr. Reed was a son of Dr. Robert R. Reed, and was born near Washington, Pa., September 28, 1832. He graduated at Washington College in 1851, taught in Georgia in 1852 and 1853, graduated at the Western Theological Seminary in 1856, and was licensed by the Presbytery of Washington on the 17th of April of the latter year. He subsequently spent a fourth year at the seminary.

The degree of "Doctor of Divinity," was conferred upon him by the College of New Jersey, at Princeton, in 1865. He has been a member of all the boards of the church, except that of Church Extension, and is one of the trustees of the General Assembly.

On the question of the union of the two branches of the Presbyterian Church, Mr. Reed took decided ground from the first agitation of the subject, and was an ardent advocate of all measures tending to promote that object. He presided at the meeting of ministers and elders which called the great convention of all branches of the Presbyterian family held in Philadelphia in September, 1867. and (with others) called and addressed the first meeting held in the country in favor of the basis adopted by the General Assemblies of the two branches in 1868. This meeting was held in the Central Presbyterian Church in Philadelphia.

In March, 1861, thirty-six members of this church, received certificates of dismission to connect themselves with churches in Harrisburg. This was occasioned by the removal of the workshops of the Pennsylvania Railroad from Parkesburg to Harrisburg.

During the year following Mr. Reed's removal to Philadelphia, the pulpit was vacant. Rev. Alfred H. Kellogg and Rev. Frederick H. Wines had been successively elected as pastor, but had both declined.

On the 29th of August, 1865, a call was extended to the Rev. John J. Pomeroy, the present pastor, which was accepted by him, and he was duly installed on the 14th day of November following.

Mr. Pomeroy was born in Roxbury, Franklin county, Pa. He prepared for college at Tuscarora Academy, graduated at Lafayette College in 1857, and at Princeton Theological Seminary in 1861, and was licensed by Carlisle Presbytery on the 10th of April of the latter year.

He was ordained by the Presbytery of Lewes on the 28th of November, 1861, and installed as pastor of the church at Dover, Delaware, the pulpit of which church he had supplied from the 1st of June preceding.

He was commissioned as chaplain of the Thirty-second Regiment of Pennsylvania Volunteers (Third Pennsylvania Reserves) on September 16, 1862, and served until its term of enlistment expired, on June 17, 1864. He then became chaplain of the One Hundred and Ninety-eighth Regiment of Pennsylvania Volunteers, a newly organized regiment, containing many of the officers and men who had formerly served in the old Reserve Corps, and filled the position until the regiment was mustered out of the service at the close of the war, June 3, 1865.

During the five years of Mr. Pomeroy's pastorate, seventy-eight have been added to the church on profession of faith, and sixty-two on certificate; sixty-one have been dismissed to unite with other churches, and thirty-two have died. During the same period, forty infants and thirty-five adults have been baptized. The present number of communicants is about three hundred and twenty.

The Sunday-schools connected with the congregation are at the present time six in number, held respectively at Sadsburyville, Parkesburg, Highland, Pomeroy, Rockdale and at the church, comprising about four hundred scholars, taught by sixty-three teachers.

The libraries contain about sixteen hundred volumes. During the last four years, one hundred and two scholars have received the reward of a Bible, for having committed perfectly to memory the Shorter Catechism. This "right arm of the church," the Sabbath-school, is very fully appreciated and sustained by the members.

There has also been contributed during the past five years to the boards of the church and to kindred objects, $3,266, and for congregational purposes, $10,266. About $3,000 of this latter sum have been expended for repairs to the meeting-house, manse, and graveyard. There is an increase from year to year in the aggregate contributions. The pastor's salary is now twelve hundred and fifty dollars, besides the manse and the use of the grounds belonging to the congregation.

During the past year, the graveyard attached to this church has, at considerable expense, been thoroughly cleaned and put in excellent condition. The work is highly creditable to the present board of trustees, who certainly deserve many thanks for the intelligent and thorough manner in which they have performed their task. The time is happily passing away in which burial places have been so generally regarded with indifference, and now it is gratifying to every person of good taste and correct feeling, to find, instead of tall grass and leaning grave-stones and sunken graves, cemeteries and enclosures so neatly kept as to make them attractive as places of profitable meditation.

It is to be regretted that for want of a session-book, the names of those who officiated as ruling elders in the early history of this church cannot be fully ascertained.

We know that Arthur Park was an elder in 1724, when Mr. Boyd became pastor, and therefore one of the first elders. In 1730, Hugh Cowan was an elder and represented the church in Presbytery. Prior to 1799, the following persons were also elders, viz., Thomas Hope, Matthew Shields, William Boggs. John Park, John Fleming, Sr., Thomas Boyd, son of Rev. Adam Boyd, Joseph Cowan, William Clingan, James Glendenning, Gideon Irwin, Arthur Park, (the second elder of that name,) George Boyd, and Henry McClellan. Of these, Thomas Hope, Matthew Shields, and William Boggs were elders in the New Side church.

John Fleming, Sr., was an elder as early as 1762, and William Clingan, Esq., as early as 1770. Arthur Park (second) is first mentioned in 1778, and George Boyd and Henry McClellan in 1790.

In 1799, John Fleming, Jr., (son of John Fleming, Sr.,) Thomas Hope, (second elder of that name,) James Boyd, Adam Cowan and James Cowan were elected and ordained.

When Mr. Latta became pastor in 1810, the bench of elders consisted of John Fleming, Sr., Arthur Park, George Boyd, Henry McClellan, John Fleming, Jr., and James Cowan.

In 1812, John Smith, Esq., John G. Parke, Thomas McClellan, and John Withrow, became members of the Session; in 1821, James B. Stewart. Thomas Scott, and John Hudders; in 1824, Martin Armstrong and Capt. Thomas Stewart; in 1832, Benjamin Davis and John M. Withrow; in 1836, William Whiteside and James G. Long; in 1841, Andrew Gibson, William N. Long, and Samuel W. Scott; in 1855, Samuel Armstrong, George Richmond, and Joseph Wiley; in 1860, Oliver Gayley; and in 1868, James Morgan Rawlins, Thomas R. Hoofman, John Andrew Parke, and Samuel Walker. The four last named, with George Richmond and Oliver Gayley, compose the present bench of elders.

The office of Deacon was for many years filled by William Stewart, Thomas Maitland and Samuel Armstrong. The present deacons are John N. Chalfant, and Samuel R. Parke; elected and ordained in 1868.

Of those who have been sexton, I have the names of William Kennedy, William Andrews, Archibald Gilfillan, James Hill, —— Heyburn, Thomas Ross, Thomas McMullin, Christopher Graham, Benjamin Harley, and George Shoemaker.

An incident has been related to me, as having occurred during the incumbency of Thomas McMullin, which those of you, who recollect him, may perhaps, appreciate: On a pleasant summer day,—the church well filled and many strangers present,—Mr. Latta was somewhat annoyed by the noise made by some boys, who had congregated in the vestibule. Turning to Thomas McMullin, the sexton, who was seated near the pulpit, he said to him in a low voice, "Thomas,

I wish you would see if there are not some boys in the vestibule?" meaning, that he should admonish them to be quiet. Thomas, however, interpreting the request literally, proceeded to the door, looked into the vestibule, turned around and exclaimed, "Yes, Mr. Latta, there are lots of them!"

This church has at different times, had on its roll of members, men who occupied positions of influence in the state. Of these, I will briefly mention the following:

Col. Andrew Boyd—son of Rev. Adam Boyd—was during a part of the Revolutionary war, Lieutanant of the County of Chester; a position of much responsibility.

William Clingan, Esq., was a sterling, patriotic citizen of West Caln township. He held a commission as justice of the peace, from 1757 to 1786, and for the last six years of that period, was President of the County Courts. From 1777 to 1779, he was a member of the Continental Congress, during which period the Articles of Confederation were adopted, under which the country was governed from 1778 to 1789, when the present Constitution went into operation. In 1779, he was appointed to receive subscriptions to the resolve of Congress, for borrowing twenty millions of dollars. He left no descendants.

John Fleming, Sr., was a member from Chester County, of the convention which framed the State Constitution of 1776, and also of the Assembly of Pennsylvania in 1778.

Dr. Joseph Gardner, was an active man among the revolutionary patriots of Chester county—was a member of Assembly in the years 1776, 1777 and 1778; and was chosen a counsellor in 1779. He was also a member of the Continental Congress in 1784 and 1785. He resided on the property now owned by Richard McPherson, near Sadsburyville, and practiced his profession. His descendants rank among the most respectable citizens of our ancient county.

Joseph Park, Esq., was a member of Assembly in the years 1779, 1780, 1783, 1784, 1802 and 1807.

Stephen Cochran was a member of Assembly in 1777, and of the House of Representatives after the adoption of the new constitution in 1790.

John Gardner, a son of Dr. Joseph Gardner, was sheriff of Chester County, from 1781 to 1783, to which office he was unanimously elected. He was very active in the Revolutionary war.

Methuselah Davis was a member of the House of Representatives of Pennsylvania, in 1802, 1803, 1804 and 1805. Francis Gardiner was a member in 1803.

Samuel Cochran—descended from a family who originally belonged to this church—was a member of the House of Representatives, in 1816 and 1817, and of the Senate of Pennsylvania from 1818 to 1820. He was also Surveyor General under the administration of Governor McKean, from 1800 to 1809; and under that of Governor Hiester, from 1821 to 1824. He was a prominent man in his day, prepossessing in his appearance, held in high esteem by his neighbors, and his advice was sought by them in their difficulties. As evidence of his standing, it may be added, that he was forty years a ruling elder in the Faggs Manor Presbyterian Church.

John G. Parke was a member of the Assembly in 1818; Wallace Boyd, in 1818, 1821 and 1822; Robert Futhey, in 1841 and 1842; Robert Parke, in 1843, 1844 and 1845; and David J. Bent, in 1849, 1850 and 1851.

Robert Parke was also an Associate Judge of Chester County, by appointment of Governor Pollock, to fill an unexpired term, from May to December 1856; and by election, from December, 1858, to December, 1863.

R. Agnew Futhey, was County Superintendent of Common Schools of Chester County, from 1854 to 1857, being the first incumbent in that office.

There are doubtless other names which should be added to this list, but which are not now remembered.

This church has also given many of her sons to the ministry.

The Rev. Samuel Parke, son of Joseph Parke, Esq., was born November 25, 1788. He graduated at Dickinson College in 1809; studied divinity under the direction and instruction of Rev. Nathan Grier, of Forks of Brandywine—there being then no Theological Seminaries in the church—and was licensed by the Presbytery of New Castle, in 1813. He was ordained and installed pastor of the Slate Ridge Church, in York County, in August, 1814, and sustained that relation for forty-three years. During thirty years of this time, he was also pastor of Centre Church, giving to it, one-third of his time. He discharged the duties of the ministry with great fidelity, and to the acceptance of his congregation, until 1857, when, on account of the infirmities of age, he resigned. He died on the 20th of December, 1869, in the eighty-second year of his age. His wife was a daughter of his preceptor, Rev. Nathan Grier. His son, Rev. Nathan Grier Parke, graduated at Jefferson College, in 1840, and at the Princeton Theological Seminary in 1844; was licensed by the Presbytery of Donegal, April 30, 1843; and is now pastor of the Presbyterian Church, in Pittston, Pa. In 1867, he visited Europe, and was one of the representatives of the Old School Presbyterian Church of this country, in the Assemblies of the Free Church, and of the United Presbyterian Church of Scotland.

Rev. John F. Cowan—son of Adam Cowan—was born May 8, 1801. He first learned the printing business in Lancaster, but at the termination of his apprenticeship, entered upon studies with a view to the Christian ministry. He was a subject of the great revival which spread among the churches in 1821 and 1822. He graduated at Jefferson College in 1824; studied theology in the Seminary at Princeton, and was licensed by the Presbytery of New Castle, April 8, 1829. He soon thereafter emigrated to the West, and was ordained by the Presbytery of Missouri, in 1830. His first charges were the churches of Apple Creek and Brazeau, Missouri; to which, in 1833, Cape Girardeau was added. Here he labored until 1839, when he became pastor of the churches of Potosi and Belleview, in the same state. This connection he maintained until

1852. From 1853 to 1856, he was stated supply of the church at Washington, Mo., when he took charge of the church at Carondolet; and after the breaking out of the Rebellion, he was also chaplain of the military hospital in St. Louis. In this latter service, he incurred the disease which terminated his life on the 29th of September, 1862.

Mr. Cowan was in the fullest sense, an evangelist, "in labors abundant," and crowned with the most joyful success. He was a pioneer of the Church in Missouri, and was instrumental in founding and strengthening a number of churches.

He lived respected by all who knew him, and beloved by those who knew him best, and his name is held in grateful remembrance by hundreds of converts, who claim him as their spiritual father. He visited this congregation about 1849, and took an active part in the revival of that period; and many of the members of this church, who were brought within the fold of Christ at that time, cherish his memory with affection.

He has two sons in the ministry, the Rev. John F. Cowan and the Rev. Edward Payson Cowan, both of whom graduated at Westminster College, Missouri; and at the Theological Seminary at Princeton; and were licensed to preach by the Central Presbytery of Philadelphia—the first in 1860, and the last in 1864. Rev. John F. Cowan is now pastor of the Aux Vasse Church in Missouri, and Rev. Edward P. Cowan, of the Market Square Church in Germantown, Pa.

Rev. John Wallace—the son of Charles and Ann (Truman) Wallace—was born October 1, 1791. He was self educated, both in regard to his classical attainments and theology; and was licensed by the Presbytery of New Castle, October 4, 1826, the Presbytery, in their minutes recording his licensure, saying "his being an exceptional case." On the 5th of November, 1833, he was ordained and installed as pastor of the churches of Pequea and Cedar Grove, in Lancaster County. In 1839, Cedar Grove became a distinct charge, and his pastoral relation to that church was dissolved. He continued his connection with Pequea, until his death, October 29, 1866. He was highly esteemed by his ministerial brethren, and was known throughout the whole region of his labors, as an eminently good and faithful man.

Rev. William Pinkerton was born near Sadsburyville, pursued his preparatory studies at New London Academy, graduated at Washington College, Pa., in 1833, studied theology at Princeton Theological Seminary, and was licensed by the Presbytery of New Castle, September 10, 1839. He has been pastor successively of the Cove Church, in Albemarle County, Virginia; High Bridge Church, in Rockbridge County, Virginia, and of Collierstown Church in the same county. His present charge is Mt. Carmel, Augusta County, Virginia.

Rev. James Long Scott—son of Thomas Scott—was born October 27, 1812, pursued his preparatory studies at Moscow Academy, graduated at Jefferson College in 1833; studied theology in Princeton Seminary, from 1835 to 1838; and was ordained by New

Castle Presbytery, on September 25th of the latter year, as a missionary to the heathen.

On October 10, 1838, he sailed for India as a missionary of the Board of Foreign Missions, of the Presbyterian Church. There he labored thirteen years, at the three stations of Futtehgurh, Mynpoora and Agra. He then returned home, and after remaining a year and a half in this country, returned to India in 1853, and was stationed at Agra, until after the memorable year of the mutiny, when so many valuable lives of our missionaries were lost. He then went again to Futtehgurh, where he spent several years, and until failing health required a change of climate, when he repaired to the Himalaya mountains, and engaged in preparing a commentary on the Gospels in the Hindostani language.

His health not improving, he was advised by medical men to leave India, which he did, and returned to this country, after having spent twenty-seven years in missionary labor.

He now resides at Hammonton, New Jersey, where he conducts a Family Boarding School.

Rev. William F. P. Noble, received his academic education at the Strasburg Academy, in Lancaster County; graduated at Lafayette College in 1847; studied theology at Princeton; was licensed by the Potosi Presbytery, of South Eastern Missouri, in January, 1857; and by the same Presbytery ordained as an evangelist, in April of the same year.

He became pastor of the Presbyterian church at Belair, Maryland, within the bounds of the Presbytery of Baltimore, in October, 1858, and continued in that relation until April, 1860. From November 25th, 1862, to October 6th, 1863, he was pastor of the Upper West Nottingham Church, in this county; during the rebellion, was a chaplain in the United States Army; supplied Colerain Presbyterian Church from 1866 to 1869; and on the 13th of May of the latter year was installed by the Presbytery of New Castle as pastor of the Penningtonville Presbyterian Church.

Owing to the state of his health, Mr. Noble has employed himself largely in missionary work, laboring from place to place, as opportunity offered.

Rev. John P. Clarke, prepared for college in Rev. S. M. Gayley's Classical Institute at Wilmington, Delaware; graduated at Lafayette College in July, 1856; pursued his theological studies for two years in the Western Theological Seminary at Allegheny, and a third year at the Seminary at Princeton; was licensed by the Presbytery of New Castle April 11, 1860, and was ordained as an evangelist by the Presbytery of Huntingdon in the autumn of 1861. He labored within the bounds of the latter Presbytery as stated supply and missionary from 1861 to 1865, the first two years of which period his points of preaching were at Philipsburg, Kylertown, and Moshanon; and the last two at Moshanon, Snow Shoe, and Karthaus.

On the 29th of September, 1865, he was elected pastor of the Doe Run Presbyterian Church, in this county, where he had labored as supply from June preceding, and was installed by the Presbytery of New Castle on the 24th of May, 1866. He continued in that relation until April, 1868, since which time he has been laboring as stated supply of Little Valley Church, in Mifflin county, Pa.

Rev. John L. Withrow pursued his preparatory studies at the Tuscarora Academy, and the Media Classical Institute, graduated at Princeton College in 1857, and at Princeton Theological Seminary in 1863, and was licensed by New Castle Presbytery while still in the seminary.

His first charge was at Abington, near Philadelphia, over which he was installed in March, 1863, and where he remained until December, 1868, when he became pastor of the Arch Street Presbyterian Church in Philadelphia.

During his ministry at Abington, the contributions to the general operations of the church increased more than four fold, the membership more than doubled, the attendance was largely multiplied, and a new church edifice erected, at a cost of thirty thousand dollars, all of which was paid.

Rev. Thomas S. Long was for a time at the academies in Strasburg and Coatesville, but his classical studies preparatory to his college course, were pursued at the Tuscorora Academy. He graduated at Lafayette college July 27, 1864; spent three years in the theological seminary in Princeton, and graduated there April 23, 1867.

He was licensed by New Castle Presbytery, April 10, 1866, and was ordained and installed pastor of the church at Pequea, as the successor of Rev. John Wallace on May 7, 1867.

Mr. William Filson spent five years at the Tuscarora Academy—the last three of them as teacher—graduated at Lafayette College in 1868, entered the Western Theological Seminary the same year, and was licensed by the Presbytery of Huntingdon June 14, 1870.

Rev. James Bolton, now pastor of the Reformed (Dutch) Church at Colt's Neck, New Jersey, was a resident within the bounds of this congregation, and an attendant upon its services from 1843 to 1847, and received here religious impressions which ultimately resulted in his conversion and dedication to the Christian ministry.

He graduated at Union College, Schenectady, in 1851, studied theology at the Union Seminary in New York, and was licensed by the Presbytery of Brooklyn in 1853. For two years thereafter he occupied the position of professor of history and belles lettres in a collegiate institute in New York. He subsequently transferred his ecclesiastical relations to the Reformed (Dutch) Church, and prior to his present charge, was pastor of the Reformed Church at Fordham, New York.

In addition to these, the Rev. Samuel T. Lowrie—whose maternal grand-parents were members of this church, and who is a lineal descendant of Arthur Park, the first ruling elder—is entitled to a place in this history.

He was born in Pittsburg, February 8, 1835,

graduated at the Miami University in 1852, spent four years in the Western Theological Seminary, and was licensed by the Presbytery of Ohio, (O. S.,) January 8, 1856. He went to Germany in April, 1856, and remained there until June, 1857, residing in Heidelberg, and studying in the university at that place. He then made a pilgrimage to Syria and Palestine, and returned home in January, 1858. He was pastor of the church at Alexandria, in Huntingdon county, Pa., from December, 1858, to April, 1863, when he again spent some time in Europe. In 1864, he was with the army under General Sherman in Tennessee and Georgia, doing duty in hospitals and camps as a delegate of the Christian Commission.

In October, 1864, he went to Philadelphia, and was instrumental in building up the Bethany Mission in that city, with which enterprise he was connected until April, 1869, when he became pastor of the church in Abington, Pa., as the successor of Rev. John L. Withrow, who, as already observed, is also a descendant of Arthur Park, the first.

Mr. Edward P. Clark, a great-grandson of Rev. William Foster, is now in the Union Theological Seminary in New York, preparing for the ministry.

In this connection I may add the name of Rev. Samuel A. Gayley—a son of Mr. Daniel Gayley, a venerable and highly esteemed member of this church —who was licensed by the Presbytery of New Castle, April 11, 1849, and is now pastor of the Lower West Nottingham Church, in Cecil County, Maryland.

This church has also at different times, been the

recipient of sums of money bequeathed to it by its members.

In 1811, William Davidson bequeathed £10. This legacy—for some cause—does not appear to have ever been received.

In 1813, William Minnes, three hundred and fifty dollars, which is now invested in stock of the Philadelphia Bank.

In 1815, John Mitchell, fifty dollars for the repair of the graveyard wall. This legacy was used in rebuilding the wall when the yard was enlarged, about the year 1843.

In 1837, Eliza Ann Cairns, two hundred and forty-three dollars to discharge a debt, resting on the church building in Sadsburyville, and one hundred and fifty dollars for the support of the poor. The last named sum is invested in stock of the Pennsylvania Railroad Company.

In 1842, James Russell, fifty dollars for the repair of the graveyard well, which was used for that purpose.

In 1843, James Boyd, two hundred dollars, for the support of the Gospel. This legacy is invested in stock of the Philadelphia Bank.

In 1847, Tabitha Parke, one hundred dollars for the use of the church. This legacy was appropriated towards the payment of the debt incurred in erecting the present church building.

In 1856, Samuel Parke McClellan, bequeathed a mortgage of twelve hundred and fifty dollars and the interest unpaid thereon. By a vote of the congregation, these moneys were expended in the erection of the Manse.

In 1861, Enoch Stewart, two hundred dollars, which was expended in liquidating a portion of the debt incurred in erecting the Manse.

In 1825, Eleanor Tate bequeathed a sum of money to John G. Parke, "for his kindness," which Mr. Parke donated to the Poor Fund of the Church, and it was invested, together with the legacy of Eliza Ann Cairns—already mentioned—in Pennsylvania Railroad Stock.

I make this record of these bequests, because I feel that particular honor is due to the memory of those, who devise liberal things in the way of supporting the Church.

I have thus endeavored to trace the history of this Church, during the one hundred and fifty years which have run their course since its foundations were laid. Doubtless, many things which would have been interesting and instructive, have—for want of faithful chroniclers—passed beyond recall.

I beg leave here to suggest, that full records be hereafter kept, so that when this church, fifty years hence, shall celebrate its bi-centenary; the historian—now in his infancy, or mayhap, unborn—may find his task a comparatively light one, and be able to present its doings in the Master's vineyard in a satisfactory manner.

In this review, we see the power and sublimity of the religion of Christ. The influence of the church can never be known in time. "Its lines stretch out beyond mortal ken, observed only by the eye of the Omniscient. Who can measure the good done by this church? To comprehend it, in anything like its full measure and meaning, we must know the spiritual history of its numerous members, who generation after generation, have impressed their lives upon the world.

"The existence of a true church in a community is a power for good. There are a thousand influences which gather around the sanctuary, and the Sabbath, and the ordinances of the Church which mould the heart and shape the life, beyond what can possibly be known on earth."

Through a century and a half, this Church has had a preached Gospel, and God's grace and mercy have very many times been specially poured out in answer to the prayers of his people. "Solemn spot, where the voice of instruction, of admonition, of comfort, and of peace have been so long heard."

And that city of the dead,—through whose gateway so many of our friends have been borne, and which is filled with memorial stones, reared by the hand of affection, admonishing us of the flight of years, and the uncertainty of life, in that the sickle of time cuts down the young as well as the old—speaks to us of the importance of being in readiness for our own departure, when He, the Master, shall come and call for us.

May God's blessing ever rest upon those who worship in this sanctuary, may he protect from harm this old church of our fathers, and make all who gather within her walls, to become "holy and humble men of heart."

APPENDIX.

A.
CHURCH ORGANIZATION, 1870.

PASTOR.
REV. JOHN J. POMEROY.

RULING ELDERS.
George Richmond,
James Morgan Rawlins,
John Andrew Parke,
Oliver Gayley,
Thomas R. Hoofman,
Samuel Walker.

DEACONS.
John N. Chalfant,
Samuel R. Parke.

TRUSTEES.
George M. Boyd, *President*,
James Reid, *Treasurer*,
Robert S. Scott,
R. Agnew Futhey, *Secretary*,
J. Latta Stewart,
John Patrick,
Richard McPherson.

SEXTON.
George Shoemaker.

B.
LIST OF SURNAMES OF THE EARLIEST MEMBERS OF UPPER OCTORARA.

Persons bearing these names, were members prior to the middle of the last century.

Alison,
Blelock,
Boggs,
Boyd,
Boyle,
Clingan,

Cochran,	Kyle.	Rowan.
Cowan,	Liggett,	Sandford,
Dickey,	Lockhart.	Scott.
Filson,	Luckey,	Sharpe,
Fleming.	McAllister,	Sloan,
Gardner,	McNeil,	Smith,
Glendenning.	McPherson,	Stewart,
Hamill.	Mitchell,	Summeril,
Henderson,	Moody,	Wiley,
Heslep.	Park,	Wilkin,
Hope,	Richmond.	Wilson.
Kerr,	Robb,	

C.

PATENT FOR CHURCH LANDS.

On the 25th of May 1743, there was surveyed unto Rev. Adam Boyd, "in trust for the Presbyterian Congregation of Upper Octorara, for the use of a meeting house and burial ground," a tract of land called "Union," situate in Sadsbury township, Chester County, described as follows:

Beginning at a marked Red Oak, in a line of Adam Boyd's land, thence by lines of marked trees, the four courses and distances following, viz.: south, thirty-nine perches to a marked Spanish Oak; east, eighteen perches to a marked White Oak; south, twenty-one peaches to a post; and west thirty-eight perches to a post, in a line of Robert Cooper's land; thence by the same north, sixty perches to a post, in a line of Adam Boyd's land; thence by the same east, twenty perches to the place of beginning; containing nine acres and one hundred and thirty-eight perches, and allowance of six acres per cent. for roads, &c.

A Patent was granted for these lands on the 26th of April, 1769, to Rev. William Foster, William Clingan, Hugh Cowan, and John Fleming—who had been nominated by the congregation to receive it—to be held by them and their successors, "In trust

APPENDIX. 153

to and for the purpose of erecting and continuing a church or house of religious worship, for the use of the United Presbyterian Congregation at Octorara, in Sadsbury township, and their descendants and successors, in such manner as the same congregation for the time being, shall from time to time, order, direct and appoint, and to and for no other use or purpose whatsoever."

This Patent is recorded in the office for recording of deeds, at Philadelphia, in book I, volume 6, page 472.

D.

NAMES OF PEW-HOLDERS GIVEN ON A DRAFT OF THE OLD CHURCH.

DATE NOT KNOWN, BUT SOME TIME IN THE LAST CENTURY.

James Boyd,
Thomas Heslep,
Arthur Park,
John McPherson,
Samuel Wright,
John Fleming, (East Caln,)
George Richmond,
James Cowan,
John Fleming, Sr.,
John Fleming, Jr.,
John Morrison,
William Stewart,
Samuel Wilson,
Robert Young,
Samuel Futhey,
Joseph Park,
William Wilkin,
John Sloan,
Rebecca Fleming,
Isaac Wentz,
Hannah Kinkead,
John Pinkerton,
John Park,
Andrew Stewart,
Widow Kilpatrick,
Samuel Copeland,
Joseph Cowan,
Alexander Glendenning,
John Smith,
Thomas and John Scott,
John and Samuel Irwin,
Richard McClure,
Wallace Boyd,
William Davidson,
Jacob Good,
Henry McClellan,
Robert McClellan,
James Arthur,
William Divan,
Widow Boyd,
Sarah McKim,
George Boyd.

11

E.

LIST OF SUBSCRIBERS TO REBUILDING OF GRAVE-YARD WALL IN 1790.

Arthur Park,
Samuel McClellan,
William Davidson,
Joseph Gardner,
John Park,
Robert Withrow,
Joseph Fleming,
William Crawford,
William Allen,
Thomas Scott,
Joseph Filson,
James Grier,
Samuel Futhey,
George Boyd,
Andrew Stewart,
Henry McClellan,
Robert McClellan,
Thomas Officer,
James Glendenning,
John Fleming, Sr.,
Thomas Heslep,
John Stille,
Bryan McCune,
William Wilkin,
Thomas Hope,
John Fleming, (of East Caln,)
Alice Fleming,
Robert Hamill,
George Richmond,
Hannah Kinkead,
Adam Glendenning,
John Ramsay,
Samuel Wilson,
John Sloan,
James Boyd,
John Smith,
Gideon Smith,
William Wiley,
John McClellan,
Joseph Park,
Robert Cowan,
John G. Park,
James Keys,
William Keys,
Alexander McPherson,
David Fleming,
Samuel Boyle,
Robert McClellan,
Francis Ruth,
David Bailey,
Agnes McPherson,
James Cowan,
Adam Cowan,
Wallace Boyd,
James Thompson,
Mary Cowan,
Jane Boyd, (widow,)
Joan Wilkin,
Joseph Wilson,
Robert Forsyth,
Edward Dougherty.

F.

FIRST CALL GIVEN TO REV. JAMES LATTA.

The congregation of Upper Octorara, being on sufficient ground well satisfied with the ministerial qualifications of you, Mr. James Latta, and having good hopes from your labours and good character, that your ministrations in the gospel will be profitable to our spiritual interests, do earnestly call and desire you to undertake the pastoral office in said congregation, the three-fourths of your time, promising you, in the discharge of your duty, all proper support and encouragement and obedience in the Lord; and that you may be free from worldly cares and avocations, we hereby promise and oblige ourselves to pay to you the sum of four hundred dollars annually, in regular half-yearly payments, during the time of your being and continuing the regular pastor of this church.

In testimony whereof we have respectively subscribed our names in behalf of said congregation, this twenty-fourth day of September, Anno Domini one thousand eight hundred and ten.

This is to certify, that at a meeting of the congregation convened by previous notice, the foregoing call for Mr. James Latta was regularly and unanimously made and subscribed by said congregation, agreeably to the rule prescribed in the Constitution of the Presbyterian Church.

Sept. 25*th*, 1810.

ROBERT WHITE,
Moderator.

ARTHUR PARK,
GEORGE BOYD,
HENRY MCCLELLAN,
JOHN FLEMING, JR.,
Elders.

G.

CHARTER OF INCORPORATION OF UPPER OCTORARA CHURCH.

GRANTED BY THE SUPREME COURT OF THE STATE, MAY 5, 1812, AND ENROLLED IN THE OFFICE OF THE SECRETARY OF THE COMMONWEALTH, IN BOOK NO. 1, PAGE 94.

To all men to whom these presents shall come: know ye, that we, whose names are hereunto subscribed, being citizens of the State of Pennsylvania, and members of the Presbyterian congregation of Upper Octorara, in the County of Chester, and State of Pennsylvania aforesaid, desirous of becoming incorporated, and acquiring and enjoying the powers and immunities of a corporation or body politic in law, according to an act of the General Assembly of the Commonwealth of Pennsylvania, entitled "An Act to confer on certain associations of the citizens of the Commonwealth the powers and immunities of corporations or bodies politic in law," we do therefore, by these presents, publish and declare that we have associated, and do hereby associate ourselves together for the said purposes, by the name, style, and title of "The Congregation of Upper Octorara," under the articles and conditions following, to wit:

1st. The said subscribers, members of the said congregation and their successors, shall, according to the above recited act, become and be a corporation or body politic in law and in fact, to have continuance by the name, style and title of "The Congregation of Upper Octorara," and as such shall have full power and authority to make, have and use one common seal, with such device and inscription as they shall deem proper, and the same to break, alter or renew at their pleasure, and by the name, style and title aforesaid, be able and capable in law to sue and to be sued, plead and to be impleaded in any court or courts, before any judge or judges, justice or justices, in all manner of suits, complaints, pleas, causes, matters and demands whatsoever, and all and every matter or thing therein, to do in as full and effectual a manner as any other person or persons, or bodies corporate, within the Commonwealth

APPENDIX. 157

of Pennsylvania, may or can do, and shall be authorized and empowered to make rules, by-laws and ordinances, and do every thing needful for the good government and support of the affairs of the said congregation; provided, that the said by-laws, rules and ordinances, or any of them, be not repugnant to the constitution and laws of the United States, and the constitution and laws of the Commonwealth of Pennsylvania, or to the present instrument upon which said corporation is founded and established.

2d. The said subscribers, and other members of the said congregation, and their successors, by the name, style and title aforesaid, shall be able and capable in law to take, receive and hold all and all manner of lands, tenements, rents, annuities, franchises and hereditaments, and any sum and sums of money, and any manner and portion of goods and chattels now the property of the said congregation, or held in trust for them, or hereafter to be granted, given, or bequeathed unto them, to be employed and disposed of towards the support of the gospel, and keeping in repair the church and burial ground belonging to the said congregation, and for such other purposes as the said congregation may deem most beneficial to the interests thereof, and the will and intention of the donor: provided, the clear yearly value or income of the messuages, houses, lands and tenements, rents, annuities, or other hereditaments and real estate of the said congregation, and the interest of the money by them lent, shall not exceed the annual sum of five hundred pounds.

3d. Every man who shall hold a pew or seat in the church of the said congregation, and shall have paid the annual price thereof within two years before any annual meeting of the congregation, and who is a professor of the Presbyterian faith, and no other, shall be members of this congregation.

4th. The members of the said congregation shall meet on the first Monday in May annually, for the purpose of choosing a committee consisting of seven of their members, which committee so chosen, or a majority of them, shall have authority to enact and ordain all necessary by-laws, and to do and perform all such other matters and things as may be necessary for the benefit of the said congregation, and shall meet annually for the said purpose on the second Monday in May, at the said church, and at such other times and places as they may think proper. If in any year a committee should not be chosen agreeable to these articles, the committee chosen at the preceding election shall continue until a new election shall be held. They shall keep a minute of their proceedings, which, with a statement of their accounts, and of the funds of the congregation, shall be open to inspection at the annual meeting of the said congregation.

5th. The committee shall take care that the debts, moneys, and other property belonging, accruing, or becoming due to the congregation from time to time, be as speedily as possible fully paid, collected and secured.

6th. The names of those who present or bequeath to the congregation any money or other property, shall be recorded on the minutes of the committee.

7th. The following named persons shall be the committee until the first Monday in May next, the time of the annual meeting of the congregation, viz.: Francis Gardner, Wallace Boyd, John Fleming, of East Caln, James Boyd, Thomas Scott, Joseph Richmond, and Samuel Boyd.

II.

LIST OF TRUSTEES FROM THE INCORPORATION OF THE CHURCH IN 1812, TO THE PRESENT TIME,

WITH THE YEARS IN WHICH THEY WERE FIRST ELECTED. MANY OF THEM SERVED AT DIFFERENT PERIODS OF TIME, AND SOME OF THEM FOR SEVERAL YEARS.

1812. Francis Gardner,
    Wallace Boyd,
    John Fleming, (E. C.,)
    James Boyd,
    Thomas Scott,

1812. Joseph Richmond,
    Samuel Boyd,
1813. James Boyd, Jr.,
    Robert Futhey,
    James Fleming,

APPENDIX.

1816, Samuel Glasgow,
George W. Parke,
1819, Matthew Boyd,
Thomas Richmond,
William Noble,
1820, Enoch Stewart,
1822, Thomas Stewart,
1824, Robert Cowan,
Christopher Wigton,
1825, John Parke,
William Stewart,
1826, John M. Withrow,
George Fleming,
1827, Francis Parke,
Thomas H. Gardner,
John Richmond,
1832, Joseph C. Boyd,
Samuel W. Scott,
William Whiteside,
Samuel Parke McClellan,

1832, Francis Armstrong,
1837, John Gault,
1839, David Parke,
Sam'l D. McClellan,
1843, Samuel Jackson,
1846, Robert Hope,
1849, William Irwin,
William Fulton,
1856, Robert Parke,
J. Wilson Hershberger,
John Andrew Parke,
1862, Evan Jones,
1866, George M. Boyd,
R. Agnew Futhey,
J. Latta Stewart,
1868, James Reid,
Robert S. Scott,
Richard McPherson,
1869, John Patrick.

I.

LIST OF PERSONS BURIED IN THE OLD "NEW SIDE" GRAVEYARD,

ON THE FARM LATE OF CYRUS COOPER, DECEASED, SO FAR AS THE SAME ARE MARKED BY GRAVESTONES.

NAME.	DATE OF DEATH.	AGE.
Joseph Wilson,	June 26, 1751,	50 y.
Hugh Wilson,	January 8, 1754,	20 y.
Daniel Kerr,	May 24, 1754,	66 y.
Mrs. Jane Hamill,	August 15, 1757,	35 y.
Mrs. Jennet Wilson,	April 8, 1759,	54 y.
Mary Hamill,	September 10, 1759,	12 y.
Phebe Hamill,	September 19, 1759,	10 y.

APPENDIX.

NAME.	DATE OF DEATH.	AGE.
John Wilson,	March 4, 1760,	23 y.
John Moody,	October 26. 1766,	52 y.
Martha Hamill,	August 21, 1784,	40 y.
Joseph Wilson,	December 8, 1791,	51 y.
Andrew King,	September 28, 1800,	36 y.
Robert Hamill,	August 3, 1803,	84 y.
Mrs. Jane Hamill,	December 1, 1803,	72 y.
George Sloan,	December 30, 1803,	82 y.
Jane Boggs,	September 3, 1830,	85 y.
William Boggs,	March 4, 1833,	89 y.
Rebecca Boggs,	January 19, 1835,	84 y.
Elizabeth Boggs,	March 3, 1835,	87 y.
James Hamill,	June 24, 1836,	27 y. 4 m. 16 d.
Israel Hamill,	June 30, 1838,	61 y. 6 m. 28 d.
Israel Hamill,	June 24, 1840,	25 y. 4 m. 24 d.
Mrs. Mary Hamill,	June 21, 1861,	85 y.

K.

LIST OF PERSONS BURIED IN UPPER OCTORARA GRAVEYARD,

SO FAR AS THE SAME CAN BE ASCERTAINED.

NAME.	DATE OF DEATH.	AGE.
Margaret Allison,	September 21, 1748,	48 y.
James Allen,	July 15, 1823,	32 y. 7 m. 26 d.
George Allen,	January 15, 1828,	6 y. 1 m. 14 d.
Mary Jane Armstrong,	August 24, 1836,	4 y. 6 m. 21 d.
Mary M. Armstrong,	April 17, 1854,	34 y.
Sarah Armstrong,	May 26, 1860,	69 y. 1 m. 4 d.
John Armstrong,*	July 11, 1864,	30 y. 5 m. 16 d.
Martin Armstrong,	April 22, 1867,	76 y.

* John Armstrong died from wounds received in battle, during the War of the Rebellion. He was a member of the 21st Reg't Penna. Cav.

APPENDIX.

NAME.	DATE OF DEATH.	AGE.	
William Armstrong,	December 28, 1868,	51 y.	
Samuel Armstrong,	January 3, 1870,	72 y.	8 m.
James Armstrong.			
Francis Armstrong.			
John Boyle,	——— 1739,	22 y.	
Ann Boyle,	October 7, 1742,	46 y.	
Robert Boyd,	April, 1743,	65 y.	
Rachel Boyd,	October 30, 1748,		9 m.
John Boyd,	September 21, 1750,	45 y.	
William Boyd,	July 23, 1752,	3 y.	
Mary Boyd,	December 10, 1753,	45 y.	
William Boyd,	January 19, 1762,	55 y.	
Rev. Adam Boyd,	November 23, 1768,	76 y.	
Dorington Boyle,	November 20, 1772,	40 y.	
Margaret Boyd,	May 18, 1777,	31 y.	
Thomas Boyd, Esq.,	September 22, 1778,	45 y.	
Matthew Boyd,	May 17, 1782,	45 y.	
Col. Andrew Boyd,	March 23, 1786,	46 y.	
Agnes Blealock,	September 13, 1787,	80 y.	
James Boyd, Sr.,	June 2, 1799,	84 y.	
Catharine Boyd,	January 21, 1802,	65 y.	
Mary Boyd,	January 24, 1806,	78 y.	
William H. Boyd,	July 12, 1808,	32 y.	9 m. 22 d.
C. Maria Boyd,	January 15, 1809,	7 y.	
Isabella Barber,	February 20, 1809,	21 y.	1 m. 22 d.
John Boyd,	February 11, 1810,	23 y.	6 d.
Samuel Boyd,	April 18, 1814,	33 y.	
Elizabeth Boyd,	June 30, 1815,	35 y.	
James Boyd,	November 24, 1815,	40 y.	
George Boyd,	September 24, 1818,	76 y.	
Samuel Bryan,	October 6, 1821,	60 y.	
Mary Boyd,	March 26, 1825,	72 y.	
Mary Boyd,	April, 1825.		
Elizabeth Boyd,	January 9, 1827,	34 y.	
Michael Wallace Boyd,	November 25, 1827,	65 y.	16 d.

APPENDIX.

NAME.	DATE OF DEATH.	AGE.	
John C. Banford,	September 22, 1839,	1 y.	22 d.
Hannah Boyd,	February 23, 1840,	75 y.	
Jane Boyd,	January 1, 1843,	75 y.	
Mary Boyd.			
James Boyd,	January 23, 1843,	84 y.	
Andrew Jackson Browne,	October 13, 1847,	31 y. 11 m.	3 d.
Samuel C. Banford,	June 29, 1849,	8 y. 3 m.	19 d.
Abigail H. Boyd,	August 31, 1849,	60 y.	
George L. Blankenbeler,	December 28, 1850,	4 m.	10 d.
Sarah Boyd,	April 10, 1852,	80 y.	
Thomas W. Boyd,	April 13, 1852,	55 y. 8 m.	13 d.
James Buckley,	August 19, 1852,	7 y. 2 m.	27 d.
Robert Buckley,	January 3, 1853,	46 y.	
Ann G. Browne,	April 8, 1853,	80 y	
Andrew Browne,	October 16, 1855,	74 y. 10 m.	25 d
Edwin Babb,	May 30, 1857,	22 y.	
Mary Ann Boggs,	June 16, 1857,	21 y.	
James Buffington,	September 20, 1857,	59 y.	
Edwin F. Babb,	November 12, 1860,	3 y. 6 m.	
Charles R. Boyd,	August 14, 1861,	12 y. 1 m.	29 d.
William C. Bryan,	April 9, 1862,	66 y.	
John C. Brown,	January 10, 1864,	40 y. 2 m.	8 d.
Anna C. Babb,	April 4, 1864,	1 y. 11 m.	4 d.
Matthew Boyd,	July 3, 1865,	82 y.	
Sarah McDill Boyd,	September 26, 1865,	79 y. 2 m.	15 d.
Benjamin Brook,	September 3, 1865,	5 y. 5 m.	
John Boyd,	April 26, 1867,	63 y. 3 m.	6 d.
Maggie Brook,	June, 1869,	1 y. 8 m.	20 d.
Oliver G. Blackburn,	July 22, 1870,	3 y. 1 m.	4 d.
Ann Cowan,	March 17, 1734,	33 y.	
Susanna Cochran,	February 13, 1739,	67 y.	
Jane Cochran,	February 13, 1739,	67 y.	
John Cowan,	March 15, 1748,	21 y.	
Nathaniel Cochran,	September, 1748,	6 y.	
James Cowan,	October 1, 1751,	27 y.	

APPENDIX. 163

NAME.	DATE OF DEATH.	AGE.
Robert Cochran,	October 20, 1759,	33 y. 6 m.
Isabella Cochran,	May 12, 1760,	60 y. 4 m. 8 d.
Isabel Cochran,	February 20, 1762,	1 y. 1 m. 21 d.
David Cochran,	June 19, 1771,	61 y.
Ann Cloyd,	——— 1773,	29 y.
Hannah Cochran,	August 1, 1779,	2 y. 5 m. 18 d.
Jane Cochran,	October 26, 1783,	42 y. 8 m. 20 d.
Catharine Clingan,	February 8, 1785,	Advanced age.
William Clingan, Esq.,	May 9, 1790,	Advanced age.
Rebecca Cochran,	June 5, 1790,	29 y. 4 m. 19 d.
Stephen Cochran,	November 1, 1790,	57 y. 11 m. 14 d.
David Cochran,	April 3, 1794,	6 y. 7 d.
Margaret Cochran,	September 1, 1794,	7 y.
James Cochran,	April 11, 1800,	1 y. 11 m. 26 d.
Margaret Cochran,	May 12, 1802,	85 y.
James Cochran,	September 7, 1804,	37 y.
Elizabeth Cairns,	June 3, 1810,	48 y. 2 m. 3d.
James Cochran,	December 12, 1812,	74 y.
Elizabeth Cowan,	November 26, 1814,	28 y.
James Mitchel Cochran,	August 17, 1814,	24 y. 7 m. 12 d.
Margaret Cunningham,	November 10, 1816,	3 y. 8 m.
Elinor Cunningham,	March 4, 1819,	84 y.
Samuel Cairns,	April 21, 1822,	48 y.
Margaret Cooper,	May 1, 1824,	27 y. 6 m.
Infant son of Margaret Cooper,	June 30, 1824,	2 m. 16 d.
Mary Ann Cooper,	December 10, 1824,	2 y. 8 m. 10 d.
David Cochran,	June 21, 1825,	73 y. 2 m. 9 d.
Susan Cochran,	November 17, 1825,	64 y.
Martha Cochran,	April 11, 1826,	75 y.
Samuel Cochran,	May 3, 1829,	66 y. 3 m. 17 d.
James H. Cochran,	January 2, 1830,	33 y.
Hannah Cowan,	March 9, 1831,	29 y. 10 m. 4 d.
Susanna Cochran,	November 21, 1833,	44 y. 2 m. 10 d.
David Cochran,	August 14, 1835,	35 y. 4 m. 19 d.
Robert Cochran,	November 1, 1835,	86 y.

APPENDIX.

NAME.	DATE OF DEATH.	AGE.
John Cunningham,	December 11, 1835.	91 y. 3 m.
Eliza Ann Cairns,	February 4, 1837,	28 y.
Jane Cochran,	March 9, 1838,	76 y.
Amos Cowan,	August 9, 1842.	6 y. 3 d.
Mary Ann Cowan,	September 19, 1842,	17 y. 10 m. 8 d.
Mary Ellen Crawford,	July 25, 1844,	1 y. 24 d.
Alpheus Cooper,	February 21, 1845,	56 y. 1 m. 21 d.
Hannah Cochran,	August 16, 1847.	84 y.
James Cowan,	November 18, 1850,	83 y. 6 d.
William Cowan,	September 8, 1853,	60 y. 2 m. 4 d.
Mary Cowan,	March 11, 1855,	80 y. 9 m.
Henry Cosgrave,	April 27, 1855,	59 y.
Margaret A. Cunningham,	June 24, 1864.	51 y. 11 m. 4 d.
Geo. Fleming Cowan,	January 19, 1865,	39 y. 10 m. 16 d.
Wendel Creamer,	December, 1865,	
John Chapman,	July 26, 1867,	56 y.
—— Cook,	April, 1869,	
Willie F. Clark,	March 24, 1869,	6 y. 8 m. 7 d.
James F. Cowan,	September 30, 1869,	41 y. 2 m. 23 d.
John Cochran,		
Martha Dickey,	—— 1762,	48 y.
Wm. G. Daniel,	September 26, 1826.	2 y. 5 m.
John Daniel,	September 27, 1826,	28 y.
Joshua Davis,	May, 1831.	
Rachel Darlington,	March 13, 1848.	30 y. 1 m. 4 d.
Eliza Dean,	December 30, 1850,	54 y.
Anna Mary Dorland,	July 25, 1851.	5 y.
Edw. F. Gay Darlington,	September 30, 1852,	6 m. 15 d.
James L. Dorland,	November 7, 1852.	2 y. 9 m.
Jacob Dean,	May 9, 1854,	73 y.
John P. Daniel,	October 22, 1856.	30 y. 2 m.
Maggie Bell Daniel,	October 28, 1856,	9 m. 8 d.
Robert Dorland,*	November 2, 1861,	20 y.

* Robert Dorland was a member of Company B, 97th Regiment Pennsylvania Volunteers, in the War of the Rebellion, and died from disease contracted in the service.

APPENDIX.

NAME.	DATE OF DEATH.	AGE.
Sarah Drake,	September 5, 1862.	41 y. 10 m. 25 d.
John P. Dorland,	December 21, 1865,	60 y.
Wm. Kennedy Davis,	April 9, 1866,	64 y. 11 m. 11 d.
Howard Darlington,	December 7, 1867,	6 y.
Malinda M. Darlington,	May 22, 1870,	51 y.
Mary Ann Davis,	no date,	18 y. 4 m. 25 d.
Elizabeth Jane Davis,	no date,	12 y. 2 d.
Rachel Reed Davis,		1 y. 9 m. 17 d.
John Darlington,	September, 1870,	20 y.
Infant son of Wm. K. and Jane Davis,		
Margaret Fleming,	August 9, 1754,	48 y.
Margaret Fleming,	June 6, 1767,	28 y. 9 m. 18 d.
James Fleming,	May 3, 1767,	64 y.
Henry Fleming,	June 12, 1776,	31 y.
Rev. William Foster,	September 30, 1780,	41 y.
David Fleming,	April 5, 1784,	73 y.
Margaret (McPherson) Futhey,	September 25, 1784,	27 y.
William Fulton,	March 2, 1785,	56 y.
Susanna Fulton,	———1792,	60 y.
Mary Fleming,	April 5, 1797,	40 y.
Joseph Fleming,	April 28, 1799,	61 y. 2 m.
Ann Fleming,	February 10, 1810,	44 y. 4 m.
Joseph Filson,	December 24, 1811,	57 y.
Lilley Filson,	November 3, 1812,	51 y.
Amos Fleming,	July 22, 1812,	
John Fleming, Sr.,	September 2, 1814,	83 y.
David Fleming,	February 14, 1815,	45 y.
Joseph Fleming,	September 12, 1816,	41 y. 8 m. 4 d.
Abigail Fleming,	December 8, 1816,	17 y.
Abigail Fleming,	October 2, 1818,	77 y.
Elizabeth Fleming,	March 29, 1819,	55 y.
Rebecca Fleming,	October 16, 1821,	82 y.
Mary Fulton,	September 1, 1824,	34 y. 9 m. 11 d.
Julian Filson,	——— 1826,	

APPENDIX.

NAME.	DATE OF DEATH.	AGE.
Martha Futhey,	August 16, 1827,	73 y. 5 m. 8 d.
Martha Elizabeth Futhey,	May, 1828,	3 m.
John Fleming, of E. Caln,	June 16, 1830,	69 y. 1 m. 9 d.
Margaret Fleming,	March, 1830.	
John Fleming, Jr.,	December, 1832.	
Sarah Jane Fulton,	July 11, 1833,	1 y. 3 m.
John Smith Futhey,	October 7, 1836,	Infancy.
Lucinda A. Fleming,	August 9, 1841,	24 y. 8 m. 15 d.
Martha Ann Fulton,	May 6, 1843,	7 y. 4 m.
Margaret E. Fulton,	May 11, 1843,	3 y. 5 m.
Benjamin A. Fulton,	May 17, 1843,	5 y. 5 m.
Sarah Futhey,	November 29, 1844,	52 y. 8 m. 19 d.
John W. Filson,	—— 1847.	
Samuel S. Finney,	August 8, 1848,	33 y. 11 m. 18 d.
David A. Fleming,	December 9, 1850,	38 y. 10 m. 29 d.
Joseph Filson,	September 17, 1851,	83 y. 6 m. 17 d.
Susanna M. Filson,	—— 1850.	
Elizabeth Fulton,	August 18, 1853,	2 y. 7 m.
Tabitha Fleming,	October 27, 1855,	8 y. 3d.
Samuel Futhey,	March 29, 1855,	61 y. 1 m. 24 d.
Samuel Finney,	March 27, 1856,	76 y. 7 m. 7 d.
Mary Filson,	April 30, 1858,	44 y.
Ella Finney,	September 1, 1858,	6 m.
Margaret Futhey,	April 11, 1864,	72 y. 8 m.
Preston M. Fleming,	March 8, 1864,	50 y.
Mary Lizzie Fielis,	February 6, 1865,	1 y. 2 m. 9 d.
Catharine N. Finney,	September 13, 1865,	27 y. 9 m. 9 d.
John Andrew Fielis,	July 15, 1866,	4 y. 8 m. 27 d.
Francis A. Finney,	February 6, 1867,	28 y. 3 m. 4 d.
M. Eliza Futhey,	August 22, 1867,	27 y. 3 m. 28 d.
Susanna Frederick,	September 3, 1867,	19 y. 7 m. 1 d.
Franklin Filson,	April 11, 1868,	53 y.
Robert Futhey,	July 29, 1870.	81 y. 6 m. 8 d.
James Glendenning,	April 10, 1799,	81 y. 3 m.
Isabel Glendenning,	March 4, 1810,	92 y.

APPENDIX.

NAME.	DATE OF DEATH.	AGE.	
Adam Glendenning,	June 8, 1812,	66 y.	25 d.
Joseph Glendenning,	November 27, 1812,		
David Gilfillan,	January, 1819.		
Lydia Gilfillan,	——— 1820.		
Archibald Gilfillan,	——— 1821.		
Jane Gibson,	May 30, 1830,	28 y.	
George Goudy,	October 30, 1834,	65 y.	
Samuel Gibson.	March 22, 1835,	77 y.	
Matilda M. Griffith,	April 5, 1838,	32 y.	
Elizabeth Gibson,	September 8, 1838,	29 y.	
Joseph Gayley,	February 18, 1843,	24 y.	
Margaret Gayley,	September 29, 1843,	28 y.	
Elizabeth Gibson,	February 28, 1847,	67 y.	
Willie Green,	January 25, 1857,	1 y. 11 m. 26 d.	
James Garret,	January 9, 1859,	40 y.	
Emmor E. J. Gibson,	June 3, 1860,	5 y. 9 m. 16 d.	
Frances J. Gibson,	June 6, 1860,	2 y. 9 m. 7 d.	
John A. Gibson,	June 9, 1860,	8 y. 6 m. 23 d.	
Josiah D. Guthrie,	August 24, 1864,	26 y. 4 m. 19 d.	
Infant son of James and Martha Gormley.			
John Henderson,	August 29, 1745,	41 y.	
Thomas Heslep,	July 29, 1764,	83 y.	
Mary Heslep,	August 21, 1767,	83 y.	
Jennet Hope,	December 9, 1771,	70 y.	
Thomas Hope,	October 24, 1776,	75 y.	
Jane Heslep,	April 20, 1801,	18 y.	
William Hutten,	November 29, 1802,	6 y.	
Robert Heslep,	December 29, 1806,	27 y.	
John Ferguson Hamill,	(at sea,) 1807,	26 y.	
John Parker Ham,	July 10, 1813,	4 m. 8 d.	
Elizabeth Hamill,	September 14, 1813,	52 y.	
Richard Hope,	February 12, 1815,	42 y. 8 m.	
John Henderson,	August 29, 1815,	41 y.	
Mary Hershberger,	August 12, 1822,	71 y. 5 m. 12 d.	
Thomas Hope,	August 15, 1825,	60 y. 7 m. 3 d.	

APPENDIX.

NAME.	DATE OF DEATH.	AGE.	
Margaret Hershberger,	June 10, 1825,	52 y.	1 d.
Jane Hershberger,	September 8, 1828,	23 y. 11 m.	12 d.
David Hindman,	July 3, 1830.		
Martha Hindman,	July 19, 1830,	52 y.	
Jane Hamill,	March 19, 1831,	39 y. 4 m.	11 d.
Edwin Hershberger,	January 15, 1834,	1 y. 9 m.	2 d.
Francis Hoffman,	May 2, 1835,	76 y.	
Joseph Hudders,	October 8, 1837,	1 y. 6 m.	
Samuel Hershberger,	October 20, 1838,	73 y. 9 m.	20 d.
Sarah Hope,	October 31, 1838,	38 y. 8 m.	
William Hope, M.D.,	February 4, 1839,	29 y. 6 m.	
Mary Hope,	May 6, 1841,	19 y.	26 d.
Anna M. Hope,	December 29, 1842,	29 y. 2 m.	23 d.
Joseph F. Hoffman,	July 8, 1842,	9 y.	
Catharine Hudders,	October 15, 1842,	2 y.	
Sarah Hudders,	October 21, 1842,	3 y.	28 d.
Sarah Hope,	July 31, 1843,	36 y.	
David Hope,	November 19, 1843,	15 y. 9 m.	20 d.
Cecelia Ann Hamill,	May 7, 1843,	1 y. 5 m.	20 d.
James C. Hershberger,	September 21, 1843,	15 y. 1 m.	24 d.
Ambrose W. Hudders,	August 4, 1844,	1 y.	
Mary Louisa Hamill,	September 10, 1844,	2 y. 10 m.	
Hannah Jane Hamill,	February 18, 1845,	10 m.	11 d.
Edwin L. Hamill,	July 10, 1847,	9 m.	14 d.
Edwin Jefferies Hipple,	September 6, 1848,	10 m.	16 d.
Pamela Hershberger,	September 22, 1849,	44 y. 1 m.	14 d.
Thomas Hope,	November 26, 1849,	16 y.	
Mary Hope,	March 30, 1850,	83 y.	
Mary Hallowell,	December 28, 1850,	63 y.	
John Hershberger,	May 28, 1853,	84 y. 11 m.	11 d.
Thomas H. Hope,	May 28, 1853,	57 y. 4 m.	11 d.
Sarah J. Hope,	March 29, 1854,	22 y. 5 m.	
Elizabeth Hodgson,	July 19, 1855,	59 y.	
Annabell Hunter,	August 1, 1857,	1 y. 2 m.	6 d.
Buchanan Hoffman,	April 17, 1858,	1 y. 5 m.	17 d.
Ann Eliza Hershberger,	September 4, 1858,	28 y. 10 m.	14 d.

APPENDIX.

NAME.	DATE OF DEATH.	AGE.
Matthew S. Hamill,	August 25, 1860,	48 y.
Mrs. Jane E. Hamill,	March 19, 1861,	37 y. 14 d.
Mary Ellen Hamill,	October 31, 1861,	5 y. 7 m. 2 d.
Martha H. Hershberger,	November 6, 1861,	66 y. 11 m. 12 d.
Matthew S. Hamill,	December 11, 1861,	1 y. 4 m. 1 d.
Joseph Hope,	July 12, 1863,	57 y. 9 m. 12 d.
Samuel Hoffman,	April 22, 1864,	54 y.
Ann Hoffman,	September 18, 1864,	52 y. 11 m. 8 d.
James Hamilton,	December 12, 1866,	51 y.
Rich'd Franklin Hamilton,	——— 1867,	1 y.
Sarah Jane Hawks,	January, 1868,	2 y.
Kate E. Hoover,	March 15, 1870,	28 y.
Rich'd Franklin Hamilton,	——— 1870,	3 y.
James Hamill,	no date,	7 y.
Nancy Hamill,	no date,	7 y.
Two infant daughters of George and Catharine Hoffman,	no date.	
Dorington B. Irwin,	April, 12, 1801,	9 y. 8 m.
Mary Eliza Irwin,	October 11, 1842,	5 y. 3 m. 23 d.
Alexander M. Irwin,	September 23, 1845,	9 m. 6 d.
William T. Irwin,	November 30, 1851,	5 y. 7 m.
Louisa S. Irwin,	March 13, 1852,	10 m. 15 d.
John A. Irwin,	March 27, 1854,	1 y. 2 m. 9 d.
William Irwin,	July 31, 1856,	3 m. 5 d.
Mary A. Irwin,	August 9, 1857,	18 y.
George Irwin,	February 21, 1859,	51 y. 10 m. 2 d.
William Irwin,	January 18, 1860,	48 y. 2 m. 23 d.
James M. Irwin,*	December 3, 1864,	24 y.
Mary Irwin,	March 24, 1865,	52 y. 10 m. 27 d.
Robert Irwin,	December 5, 1865,	24 y. 9 m. 5 d.
George T. Irwin,	August 16, 1867,	2 y. 5 d.

* James M. Irwin was a corporal in Company E, 201st Reg't Penna. Volunteers, in the War of the Rebellion, and was killed by the accidental discharge of a musket in the hands of a comrade.

170 APPENDIX.

NAME.	DATE OF DEATH.	AGE.
Edith F. Irwin,	August 11, 1868,	1 y. 5 m. 17 d.
William R. Irwin.	October 17, 1868,	31 y. 9 m. 5 d.
Edith May Irwin.	March 13, 1870.	1 y. 1 m. 21 d.
Andrew Mitchell Jordan,	March 11, 1813,	29 y.
Sarah Jordan,	January 27, 1814,	56 y.
Frances Ann Jordan,	October 22, 1815,	28 y. 7 m. 10 d.
Elizabeth Jordan,	August 15, 1816,	24 y. 2 m. 28 d.
Sarah Jordan,	May 19, 1818,	32 y. 8 m. 19 d.
Hugh Jordan, Jr.,	May 12, 1820,	20 y. 4 m. 1 d.
Jane Jack,	August 5, 1821,	50 y.
Hugh Jordan,	April 14, 1828,	75 y.
John R. B. Jaquette,	September 5, 1846,	17 y.
Sarah Johnson,	July 4, 1852.	68 y.
Samuel J. Johnston,	August 30, 1856.	1 y. 2 m. 17 d.
Eliza Jane Jaquette.	June 11, 1859,	54 y. 6 m. 20 d.
Morris D. Jaquette,	no date.	1 y. 8 m.
John Andrew Jones.	November 22, 1862,	4 y. 3 m. 28 d.
Samuel Johnson,	December 24, 1867,	30 y.
——— Jakeman,	September, 1866,	infant.
——— Jakeman,	July, 1868,	infant.
Sallie E. Jones,	November 29, 1868,	22 y. 3 m.
Charles Kinkead,	December 29, 1782,	45 y.
William Kennedy.	——— 1821,	79 y.
Martha Kennedy,	——— 1825,	83 y.
Abraham Kendig,	October 22, 1834,	48 y.
John Kendig,	December 25, 1834,	46 y.
Hannah Kinkead,	——— 1835.	
Ann Kerns,	November 19, 1843,	
John Kenworthy,	July 9, 1847,	62 y. 5 m. 3 d.
Hannah Kenworthy,	December 11, 1847,	61 y. 11 m.
Jane Kinkead,	June 12, 1849,	70 y.
John P. Kendig,	August 7, 1851,	11 y. 8 m. 23 d.
Jane Kendig,	April 3, 1866,	43 y.
Mary Kendig,	no date.	

APPENDIX. 171

NAME.	DATE OF DEATH.	AGE.
Alexander Luckey,	April, 27, 1747,	30 y.
James Lockhart,	May 21, 1748,	34 y.
George Liggitt.	June 27, 1760,	50 y.
Rev. Francis A. Latta.	April 23, 1834,	67 y. 11 m. 26 d.
Hamilton Lockhart,	April, 1835.	
Mary Latta,	August 2, 1837,	65 y. 6 m. 26 d.
Elizabeth Latta,	November 10, 1840,	58 y. 9 m. 26 d.
Jane Latta,	June 20, 1841,	48 y. 7 m. 22 d.
Margaret R. H. Latta,	April 6, 1846,	21 y. 2 m. 22 d.
Margaret A. Latta,	July 23, 1848,	71 y. 11 m. 25 d.
Alexander Laverty,	December 26, 1848,	69 y.
Isabella Lockhart,	——— 1849.	
John Linn,	November 1, 1849,	25 y. 10 m. 21 d.
James M. Latta,	December 25, 1851,	45 y. 4 m. 6 d.
Clement Levis,	July 9, 1853,	59 y. 6 m. 5 d.
Margaret W. Linn,	November 28, 1857,	1 y. 6 m. 25 d.
Rev. James Latta,	May 30, 1862,	75 y. 1 m. 6 d.
Lydia Lincoln,	March 15, 1863,	21 y. 5 m.
Mary Linn,	January 18, 1869,	73 y. 11 m. 18 d.
Emma Lena Linn,	September 3, 1869,	2 y. 6 m. 16 d.
Archibald McNeil,	December 24, 1742,	43 y.
John McPherson,	December 9, 1762,	67 y.
Margaret McAlister,	November 16, 1768,	67 y.
Jane McPherson,	——— 1771.	
Robert McPherson,	——— 1777.	
Andrew Mitchel,	December 9, 1782,	54 y.
Jane Mitchel,	February 27, 1797,	23 y. 5 m. 20 d.
Alexander McPherson,	——— 1797.	
Mary McPherson,	——— 1797.	
Frances Mitchel,	August 14, 1801,	64 y.
Jane Mitchel,	June 28, 1805,	71 y. 3 m. 12 d.
Joseph L. McClellan	July 14, 1805.	7 m.
Samuel McClellan,	December 9, 1807,	75 y. 10 m.
Mary McKim,	December 21, 1807,	26 y. 7 m.
Rev. Alexander Mitchel,	December 6, 1812,	81 y.

APPENDIX.

NAME.	DATE OF DEATH.	AGE.	
Wiliam Minnes.	March 31, 1813,	80 y.	
Mary Mulhollen.	May 1, 1813,	45 y.	
John McClellan.	November 5, 1813,	47 y.	
Thomas Maitland.	in War of 1812,	86 y.	
Jane McClellan.	November 19, 1813,	66 y.	4 m. 11 d.
George Mitchel.	June 16, 1814,	54 y.	
James Mitchell, son of Andrew Mitchell.			
Robert Moore,	April 5, 1815,	40 y.	
John Mitchel.	August 16, 1815,	53 y.	
James McKown.	November, 1815.		
Margaret Moore.	June 5, 1816,	2 y.	21 d.
Ann McElwain.	April 30, 1817,	95 y.	5 m. 26 d.
John Mitchel,	July 26, 1818,	19 y.	6 m. 18 d.
Robert McClellan,	November 6, 1818,	56 y.	
Permela McPherson,	——— 1819,	16 y.	
Deborah McClellan,	May 16, 1820,	20 y.	1 m. 13 d.
Mary A. McClellan,	April 6, 1820,	23 y.	2 m. 17 d.
Henry McClellan,	September 6, 1821,	72 y.	
Josiah I. McKim,	August 18, 1822,	14 y.	9 m. 4 d.
John McPherson,	June 22, 1822,	60 y.	
Nancy McPherson.	——— 1822,	12 y.	
Thomas F. McClellan,	April 22, 1822,	1 y.	
William McNeil,	——— 1823,	65 y.	
John M. McClellan.	January 15, 1824.		
Henry McConaughy,	October 1, 1824,	10 y.	
Richard McClure,	May 30, 1824,	56 y.	5 m. 28 d.
John C. McCoy.	April 25, 1826,	50 y.	
William F. Mitchell, M.D..	September 6, 1826,	47 y.	2 m. 11 d.
Elizabeth McClellan,	December 13, 1829,	49 y.	
Elizabeth Mackey.	April 21, 1831,	78 y.	
Ann McKim.	November 28, 1832,	65 y.	
Hannah McClellan,	August 1, 1833,	68 y.	
Sarah Ann Miller,	December 12, 1833,	3 y.	23 d.
Joseph McClellan,	October 14, 1834,	87 y.	5 m. 16 d.
Thomas McClellan,	December 18, 1834,	61 y.	
Elizabeth McKim,	February 3, 1835,	44 y.	4 m.

APPENDIX. 173

NAME.	DATE OF DEATH.	AGE.
Alexander McPherson,	March, 1836,	61 y.
Rebecca McPherson,	——— 1836,	58 y.
Uree McPherson,	——— 1836,	14 y.
Frances McDonald,	June 12, 1839,	37 y.
Jane McBride,	June, 1839.	
Jane Mackey,	September 12, 1839,	89 y.
Mary McClellan,	March 4, 1841,	75 y.
Eleanor McPherson,	April 10, 1841,	79 y.
Thomas McKim,	May 10, 1841,	44 y.
Rebecca Martin,	October 30, 1841,	76 y.
Ann McClellan,	February 7, 1842,	96 y.
Janet McCaughey,	March 16, 1842,	68 y.
Joseph S. Myers,	September 25, 1842,	infant. 25 d.
Kezia McClellan,	July 21, 1842,	75 y. 6 m.
Duncan MacGregor,	August 11, 1843,	78 y.
Catharine McCorkle,	June 15, 1843,	74 y.
Martha B. Murphey,	January 13, 1844,	48 y. 11 m.
Mary Ann Mann,	May 8, 1844,	50 y. 2 m. 27 d.
Mary McConaughy,	May 15, 1845,	63 y.
Uree H. McPherson,	March 31, 1843,	2 y. 2 m.
John McKinney,	July 24, 1845,	3 m. 12 d.
Samuel Miller,	December 14, 1845,	82 y.
Mary McNaught,	February 17, 1846,	16 y. 4 m. 23 d.
Thomas L. McClellan,	November 3, 1846,	2 y. 1 m. 12 d.
Nathaniel McCaughey,	May 11, 1847,	81 y.
Elizabeth McNaught,	November 9, 1847,	22 y. 3 m. 1 d.
Capt. William McKim,	December 20, 1847,	81 y.
Sarah McClure,	January 25, 1848,	74 y.
Elizabeth McAlister,	——— 1849,	77 y.
Joseph McDonald,	May 9, 1849,	44 y.
Mary McKinney,	March 15, 1849,	41 y.
Russell McKim,	October, 1849.	
David A. McClellan,	February 20, 1850,	3 y. 8 m. 18 d.
Alonzo P. Middleton,	July 30, 1851,	2 y. 3 m.
James Middleton,	July 19, 1851,	66 y.
Phebe Marony,	August 15, 1851,	27 y. 15 d.

NAME.	DATE OF DEATH.	AGE.	
D. Thompson Murphey,	September 18, 1851,	3 y.	3 m.
Joseph P. McClellan,	February 26, 1851,	56 y.	
R. H. McFarlan,	June 6, 1851.	17 y.	1 m. 28 d.
Hannah Maria McMewes.	—— 1852,	18 y.	2 m. 11 d.
Elizabeth McKim,	January 25, 1852,	3 y.	7 m. 25 d.
Samuel Miller,	January 6, 1852,	23 y.	5 m. 8 d.
Samuel W. McClellan,	July 19, 1852,	54 y.	2 m. 19 d.
Mary E. McClellan,	May 24, 1853,	31 y.	
John D. McClellan,	September 2, 1853,	50 y.	8 m. 13 d.
William McNeil.	—— 1853,	95 y.	
Jas. McNaught Mennick,	April 13, 1853,	2 y.	11 m. 23 d.
Margaret McNaught,	August 31, 1853,	61 y.	
Mary E. McClellan.	September 6, 1854,	59 y.	2 m. 18 d.
Richard H. Maitland,	March 7, 1855.	45 y.	6 m.
Catharine McFarlan,	November 13, 1855,	53 y.	
Esther McNaught,	April 26, 1856,	28 y.	6 m. 3 d.
Alice McClellan,	April 29, 1856,	75 y.	
Samuel Parke McClellan,	May 21, 1856,	64 y.	7 m. 11 d.
Sam.Withrow McPherson.	April 18, 1856,	3 y.	8 m. 4 d.
Uree McPherson,	March 3, 1856,	6 y.	
William McConaughey.	April 13, 1858,	51 y.	
James McConaughy,	September 27, 1858,	81 y.	
James Marion McFarlan,	October 30, 1858,	30 y.	7 m. 11 d.
Jane Brownlee McCoy,	February 28, 1860,	73 y.	2 m.
Reuben Miller,	March 7, 1860,	64 y.	8 m. 23 d.
Joseph E. N. McClellan,	August 4, 1860,	4 y.	10 m. 24 d.
William McAlister,	September 14, 1860,	65 y.	6 m. 29 d.
Eliza Fleming Mitchel,	December 22, 1860,	67 y.	8 m. 10 d.
John Mellon,	November 22, 1861,	33 y.	
Jemima McNeil,	January 2, 1861,	77 y.	
J. Rambo McKim,	March 7, 1862,	11 y.	7 m.
William McAlister,*	March 7, 1863,	35 y.	4 d.
Alexander McNaught,	October 9, 1863,	31 y.	9 m. 28 d.
Maria McClellan,	March 20, 1864,	65 y.	

* William McAlister was a member of Co. K, 5th Regiment U. S. Artillery, and died at home from disease contracted in the army.

APPENDIX. 175

NAME.	DATE OF DEATH.	AGE.
Sallie Middleton,	January 3, 1864,	71 y.
Margaret MacGregor,	March 14, 1864.	80 y.
Frances B. McClellan,	May 21, 1864,	63 y. 3 m.
Lydia Miller,	October 29, 1865.	58 y. 7 m.
Dr. Jos. Gillies McNaught,	August 22, 1866,	25 y. 9 m. 9 d.
Sarah McPherson,	March 20, 1866.	62 y. 4 m.
Nancy McNaught,	August, 1866,	67 y.
John Miller, Esq.,	March 16, 1868.	72 y.
Margaret McClellan,	February 4, 1868,	71 y.
Kate McAlister,	September 5, 1868,	30 y. 2 m. 10 d.
Joseph B. McMichael,	August 22, 1869,	16 y. 10 m.
David McFarlan,	November 19, 1869,	76 y. 5 m. 23 d.
Amos M. Miller,	June 26, 1870,	72 y. 8 m. 24 d.
Robert Henry McPherson,	September 7, 1870.	4 m. 2 d.
E. McAlister,	no date.	
James Mitchell,	no date.	
Eliza McAloman,	January 5, 1871.	63 y.
James C. Noble,	December 1, 1813.	10 m. 18 d.
Christiana Noble,	January 18, 1814.	3 y. 7 m. 21 d.
Mary Ann Noble,	May 9, 1825,	2 y. 2 m. 25 d.
Nancy Agnes Noble,	June 14, 1826,	23 d.
Mary Nyce,	June 14, 1836,	58 y. 7 m.
William Noble,	February 25, 1850.	70 y. 6 m. 8 d.
Susan Noble,	January 6, 1844.	62 y. 8 m. 10 d.
John W. Osmond,	August 30, 1853,	31 y. 3 m. 9 d.
Martha C. Osmond,	September 23, 1865.	40 y.
Arthur Park,	February, 1740.	} earliest of the
Mary Park, his wife,	no date.	} name.
John Park,	July 28, 1787.	81 y.
Elizabeth Park,	May 21, 1794,	82 y.
Rachel Parke,	July 11, 1803,	24 y. 7 m. 15 d.
Letitia Park,	November 13, 1806.	2 y. 1 m. 13 d.
Jannet Park,	April 4, 1814,	77 y. 10 m.

APPENDIX.

NAME.	DATE OF DEATH.	AGE.		
Mary F. Parke,	February 17, 1817,	17 y.	8 m.	6 d.
Jane Parke, Jr.,	January 23, 1818,	34 y.	10 m.	5 d.
Margaret Parke,	May 13, 1819,	27 y.		
Ann Park,	June 3, 1820.	71 y.		
Ann Parke,	October 3, 1821,	67 y.		
Ann Jane Park,	October 10, 1821,	1 y.	3 m.	12 d.
Arthur Park,	July 11, 1822,	85 y.	9 m.	29 d.
James Potts,	July 28, 1822,	71 y.		
Joseph Parke, Esq.,	July 2, 1823,	85 y.	6 m.	11 d.
John Park,	November 15, 1823,	84 y.		
Thomas Parke,	August 27, 1824,	62 y.		
John Franklin Parke,	August 8, 1825,	1 y.	3 m.	12 d.
John Powell,	November 8, 1826,	55 y.	7 m.	
Jane Parke,	October 14, 1832,	62 y.		
Sarah Potts,	August, 1833,	74 y.	9 m.	
John G. Parke,	October 25, 1837,	75 y.	11 m.	4 d.
Mary J. Philips,	October 6, 1839,	19 y.	5 m.	13 d.
Mary E. Philips,	November 24, 1839,		3 m.	2 d.
Winfield S. Parke,	May 10, 1843,	21 y.	6 m.	29 d.
Mary Jane Parke,	September 3, 1843,		8 m.	26 d.
Joseph G. Parke,	May 25, 1844,	48 y.	1 m.	24 d.
David Parke,	June 26, 1846,	61 y.	4 m.	3 d.
Tabitha Parke,	June 5, 1847,	73 y.		
James M. Parke,	September 16, 1848,	32 y.		
Mary B. Parke,	March 26, 1849,	87 y.		
Margaret Elvina Pine,	August 4, 1851,	26 y.	6 m.	29 d.
Samuel M. Parke,	December 1, 1854,	1 y.	2 m.	26 d.
John Parke,	April 26, 1855,	53 y.	1 m.	17 d.
"Little Jennie" Parke,	February 28, 1856,			18 d.
Agnes Sutherland Paxson,	November 16, 1856,		3 m.	20 d.
Eliza Potts,	December 16, 1856,	69 y.	2 m.	25 d.
Edmund J. Porter,	October 25, 1857,	2 y.	2 m.	26 d.
Arthur Parke,	October 31, 1858,	73 y.	5 m.	10 d.
Samuel Parke,	April 28, 1859,	63 y.	11 m.	22 d.
George W. Parke,	February 25, 1860,	79 y.	4 m.	7 d.
Annie E. Parke,	April 6, 1862,	28 y.	8 m.	27 d.

APPENDIX. 177

NAME.	DATE OF DEATH.	AGE.	
Col. James Parke,	May 15, 1862,	85 y.	7 m. 16 d.
Mary R. Parke,	June 21, 1863,	82 y.	8 m. 14 d.
Rachel Parke,	July 11, 1863,	24 y.	7 m.
Hannah L. Parke,	September 19, 1864,	16 y.	2 d.
James Powers,	October 11, 1866,	28 y.	9 m.
John Pomeroy Phillips,	July 7, 1867,		9 m. 6 d.
Thomas Pyle,	May 1, 1868,	55 y.	
Mary R. Parke,	August 11, 1868,	75 y.	5 m. 10 d.
William Parke,	April 12, 1869,	77 y.	6 m. 3 d.
Jennie Paxson,	April 16, 1870,	30 y.	5 m. 23 d.
Infant son of J. and S. Paxson,	no date.		
Nathaniel Ring,	December 10, 1766,	66 y.	
Nathaniel Ring, Jr.,	March 26, 1766,	20 y.	
James Richmond,	September 19, 1801,	22 y.	9 m.
George Richmond,	June 28, 1806,	72 y.	
Samuel Reid,	August 1, 1811,	1 y.	6 m.
Mary Reid,	November 7, 1811,		4 m. 20 d.
Twin infant sons of Thos. and Ann Robinson,	Dec. 28 and 29, 1813.		
Thomas Robinson,	October 10, 1814,	34 y.	4 d.
Ann Robinson,	February 11, 1817,	34 y.	6 m. 7 d.
Isabella Ruth,	May 27, 1812,	26 y.	
Isabella Russell,	October 2, 1813,	73 y.	
Elizabeth Russell,	March 11, 1814,	71 y.	
John Reid,	August 22, 1819,	1 y.	4 m. 5 d.
Adam Reid,	November 4, 1822,	49 y.	3 d.
Sarah Ann Richmond,	August 4, 1823,	12 y.	9 m. 15 d.
Jane Susanna Richmond,	February 20, 1824,		
Jane Russell,	September 26, 1825,	42 y.	
Francis G. Ross,	May 10, 1828,	18 y.	5 m. 23 d.
Jane Richmond,	January 22, 1830,	77 y.	
Margaret Riddell,	November 22, 1832,	22 y.	
Ephraim Russell,	January 15, 1838,	85 y.	
Rachel Ross,	October 26, 1838,	64 y.	

APPENDIX.

NAME.	DATE OF DEATH.	AGE.
John Rogers,	May 17, 1838,	53 y. 11 m. 12 d.
James Russell,	December 2, 1842,	66 y.
Anna Maria Russell,	November 22, 1843,	23 y. 9 m.
Joseph Richmond,	December 6, 1843,	68 y.
Hannah Richmond,	August 4, 1847,	69 y.
Ann Ramsey,	October 30, 1848,	64 y.
Jane Russell.	April 27, 1850,	69 y.
Elizabeth Ramsay,	December 27, 1851,	75 y.
Jane M. Richmond,	April 4, 1853,	45 y.
Margaret Ramsay,	September 22, 1855,	58 y. 5 m.
Sarah Richmond,	May 9, 1856,	72 y.
Tilton Reynolds,	June 1, 1856,	54 y. 6 m. 17 d.
Charles Robinson,	March 27, 1856,	60 y.
William Ramsey,	May 18, 1858,	83 y.
James Ramsay,	June 3, 1858,	82 y.
John N. Reid,	February 4, 1860,	9 y.
Hannah Mary Reid,	February 6, 1860,	2 y.
Annie Ramsay,	April 12, 1860,	4 y. 6 m. 2 d.
Alex. Lindsey Robinson,	October 29, 1861,	76 y.
Robert Robinson,	August 20, 1862,	76 y.
Charles Ramsay,	March 23, 1863,	53 y.
Samuel Russell,	July 19, 1863,	84 y. 10 m. 16 d.
Jane A. Richmond,	October 15, 1865,	75 y.
Rebecca H. Rogers,	April 1, 1866.	75 y. 4 m. 28 d.
Alice E. Richmond,	June 20, 1866,	40 y. 5 m. 20 d.
Robert Ramsay,	March 23, 1867,	58 y.
Josie Ramsay,	August 16, 1867,	8 m.
Rebecca Ross,	August, 1867,	72 y.
Jane Reid,	May 15, 1867.	81 y. 8 m. 10 d.
Margaret Stewart,	September 7, 1748,	38 y.
Robert Sandford,	September 7, 1765,	90 y.
John Scott,	February 16, 1777,	71 y.
Walter Stewart,	April, 1778,	advanced age.
Thomas Sharpe,	October 25, 1782,	75 y.
James Smith,	December, 1785,	66 y.

APPENDIX. 179

NAME.	DATE OF DEATH.	AGE.	
Alex. Mitchel Stewart,	June 5, 1789,	2 y.	14 d.
James McMechin Smith,	——— 1789,	1 m. 12 d.	
John Evans Smith,	——— 1793,	11 m.	
William Stewart,	August 24, 1794,	3 y.	
Elizabeth Stewart,	April 14, 1797,	24 y. 5 m. 18 d.	
Jane Smith,	September 15, 1801,	44 y. 8 m. 2 d.	
Martha Smith,	September 18, 1801,	3 y. 9 m. 13 d.	
Abraham Sides,	December 3, 1804,	10 y.	
Andrew Stewart,	December 26, 1804,	68 y.	
Thomas Scott,	September 30, 1808,	77 y.	
Sarah Smith,	July 11, 1812,	88 y.	
Agnes Stewart,	April 6, 1814,	68 y.	
Rebecca Stewart,	August 20, 1814,	36 y.	
Sarah Scott,	September 20, 1815,	76 y.	
Robert J. Shoemaker,	July 7, 1819,	1 y. 7 m. 26 d.	
John Scott,	March 8, 1824,	59 y. 4 m. 7 d.	
Elizabeth Stigers,	——— 1825,		
John Smith, Esq.,	March 19, 1829,	79 y.	
Sarah Stewart,	October 28, 1829,	57 y. 2 d.	
Sarah B. Scott,	December 15, 1829,	4 y. 6 m. 11 d.	
Ann Love Stewart,	August 31, 1830,	48 y.	
Elizabeth Shoemaker,	November 17, 1830,		
Sarah Smith,	January 15, 1831,	64 y. 11 m.	
Peter Shoemaker,	February 18, 1832,		
Mary Stewart,	July 3, 1832,	54 y.	
James B. Stewart,	November 28, 1837,	59 y.	
John Sloan,	May 10, 1840,	80 y.	
Elizabeth Scott,	March 4, 1841,	67 y.	
Dr. Jonathan H. Scholfield,	May 31, 1841,	55 y.	
Thomas Scott Stewart,	September 29, 1841,	9 y. 2 m. 23 d.	
Hannah Jane Stewart,	September 19, 1841,	13 y. 2 m. 4 d.	
Mary Stewart,	July 3, 1842,	54 y.	
Elizabeth Shoemaker,	August 18, 1842,	59 y. 6 m. 11 d.	
Margaret Sloan,	December 28, 1843,	66 y.	
Elizabeth Scholfield,	January 15, 1844,	2 y.	
D. Clinton Stackhouse,	May 22, 1844,	28 y.	
William K. Sloan,	July 10, 1844,	26 y. 10 m.	

APPENDIX.

NAME.	DATE OF DEATH.	AGE.
Joseph Scott,	April 18, 1845,	26 y. 6 m. 15 d.
George Carpenter Sloan,	July 20, 1845,	5 m. 8 d.
Amy Scott,	September 17, 1845,	19 y. 11 m. 24 d.
William Schofield,	May 17, 1848,	8 m. 12 d.
Andrew Stewart,	December 26, 1848,	68 y.
Robert Sloan,	February 24, 1851,	3 y. 9 m. 3 d.
Sarah Ann Sloan,	March 10, 1851,	1 y. 11 m. 20 d.
Amy Scott,	September 9, 1852,	69 y. 11 m. 13 d.
James Schofield,	October 26, 1852,	1 y. 7 m.
William A. Stewart,	February 28, 1853,	13 y. 6 m. 22 d.
Catharine Louisa Scott,	August 25, 1855,	2 y. 5 m.
William Stewart,	April 14, 1855,	29 y. 5 m. 3 d
John Shoemaker,	January 26, 1856,	
Margaretta Shinn,	April 23, 1856,	53 y.
Anna Schofield,	July 19, 1856,	3 y. 2 m. 3 d.
Hannah Smith,	November 20, 1856,	74 y.
James Schofield,	December 4, 1856,	45 y. 7 m.
Isabella Smith,	January 26, 1857,	91 y.
Albert Shore,	March 29, 1857,	2 y.
Eliza Ella Sloan,	June 2, 1858,	3 y. 9 m. 20 d.
Joseph Heslep Sloan,	June 7, 1858,	8 m. 17 d.
Elizabeth Y. Simpson,	May 26, 1860,	25 y. 8 m. 3 d.
Brittain G. Strickland,	August 10, 1860,	11 y. 2 m. 27 d.
Enoch Stewart,	April 7, 1861,	77 y. 9 m. 24 d.
Peter Shoemaker,	August 8, 1862,	70 y.
Rebecca Scott,	August 13, 1862,	90 y. 5 m. 9 d.
Samuel Scott Sloan,	May 24, 1862,	1 y. 12 d.
Joel L. Shoemaker,	March 25, 1863,	77 y. 6 m.
Hannah Stewart,	May 3, 1864,	78 y. 11 m. 13 d.
Miles Stewart Strickland,*	July 4, 1864,	23 y.
James Stewart,	January 26, 1865,	81 y. 10 m. 25 d.
David Strode Shoemaker,†	August 15, 1865,	29 y. 11 m. 21 d.

* Miles Stewart Strickland was killed by a sharpshooter, while on his way to the picket line. He belonged to Company B, 97th Reg't Penna. Volunteers, commanded by Colonel Guss.

† David Strode Shoemaker, was a member of Company B, in the 5th Reg't Penna. Cavalry, in the War of the Rebellion. He died from disease contracted in the army.

APPENDIX. 181

NAME.	DATE OF DEATH.	AGE.
Catharine D. Sloan,	December 7, 1865,	53 y. 7 m. 3 d.
Thomas Stewart,	May 24, 1865,	80 y. 9 m. 10 d.
William Stewart,	August 24, 1866,	74 y.
Joseph B. Scholfield,	November 7, 1866,	55 y. 10 m. 6 d.
Hannah Scholfield,	November 15, 1866,	77 y.
Susanna Stewart,	May 27, 1867,	67 y.
Mrs. Skelton,	May, 1868,	
——— Skelton,	September, 1868,	4 m.
David Scott,	November 12, 1868,	89 y. 10 m. 25 d.
John Grant Shoemaker,	no date,	7 m.
Maria Scholfield,	} Children of Joseph B. and Martha Scholfield.	
Annetta E. Scholfield,		
Ella B. Scholfield,		
James Taylor,	May 15, 1802,	1 y. 3 m. 3 d.
Charles Thompson,	February 3, 1809,	13 y. 9 m. 25 d.
Sarah W. Thompson,	March 19, 1814,	29 y. 2 m. 8 d.
John Tarrence,	February 7, 1821,	24 y. 8 m. 21 d.
Dr. John Tate,	March 28, 1821,	62 y.
Eleanor Tate,	November 12, 1825,	73 y.
Sarah W. Thompson,	May 27, 1843,	29 y. 2 m. 8 d.
Sarah Tarrence,	January 31, 1846,	51 y. 3 m. 3 d.
Joseph Tarrence,	March 20, 1847,	49 y.
Margaret Thompson,	August 10, 1853,	74 y. 5 m. 25 d.
Mary Louisa Toland,	June 22, 1858,	2 y. 3 m. 15 d.
Isaac D. Tarrence,	November 14, 1860,	66 y. 7 m. 7 d.
James Parke Turner,	March 5, 1862,	1 y. 5 m.
George Wilken,	June 21, 1764,	64 y.
Margaret Wiley,	April 19, 1772,	32 y.
William Wilken,	February 5, 1781,	11 m. 24 d.
Mary Wilken,	April 29, 1782,	4 y.
Eleanor Wilken,	August 20, 1782,	17 y. 8 m.
John Wilken,	April 13, 1788,	44 y.
Elizabeth Wiley,	August 9, 1794,	49 y.
Eleanor Wilken,	March 23, 1791,	87 y.
Jennet Wilken,	March 10, 1796,	3 y. 2 m.

APPENDIX.

NAME.	DATE OF DEATH.	AGE.
George Wilken,	September 27, 1805,	28 y. 3 m. 19 d.
William Wells,	September 16, 1806,	38 y. 7 m. 9 d.
Thomas Wallace,	October 26, 1806,	29 y. 6 m.
John Wallace,	March 2, 1802,	1 y. 7 m. 9 d.
William Wilkin,	November 4, 1804,	64 y. 4 m. 13 d.
John Wiley,	December 25, 1815,	77 y.
Isaac Wentz,	August 3, 1816,	45 y. 4 m. 12 d.
Jane Wallace,	January 8, 1821,	84 y.
John Wallace,	September 21, 1825,	70 y. 5 m. 5 d.
Eliza Wigton,	October 17, 1826,	22 y.
Charles Wentz,	December 31, 1827,	1 y. 7 m.
Infant daughter of John H. and Rebecca Wallace,	September 9, 1830,	4 m. 17 d.
Jennet Withrow,	December 29, 1830,	64 y. 8 m. 16 d.
Rebecca Wallace,	November 9, 1830,	23 y. 6 m. 17 d.
Mary Wentz,	April 21, 1830,	58 y. 9 m. 23 d.
Samuel R. Werntz,	May 30, 1833,	29 y. 10 m. 18 d.
Alice Wells,	July 26, 1831,	68 y. 1 m. 16 d.
Elizabeth Wright,	July 7, 1836,	58 y.
Margaret Wallace,	January 28, 1836,	71 y. 1 m. 17 d.
Mary Jane Wentz,	July 3, 1837,	9 y. 6 m. 23 d.
Susanna R. Wentz,	July 3, 1837,	4 y. 7 m.
Sarah B. Wentz,	November 18, 1838,	8 y. 9 m. 15 d.
John Wright, Sr.,	December 2, 1839,	59 y.
John Withrow,	October, 1840,	80 y.
Joseph Hamilton Wiley,	September 28, 1842,	5 y. 4 m. 11 d.
Margaret Wiley,	November 20, 1842,	5 y. 3 m. 20 d.
Wm. Henry Wright,	February 22, 1843,	2 y. 2 m. 25 d.
Edward S. Wiley,	September 23, 1843,	9 y.
Emma Wiley,	September 25, 1843,	4 y. 7 m. 6 d.
Mary Jane Watts,	August 22, 1844,	9 m. 8 d.
Sarah Jane Wiley,	October 20, 1844,	5 y. 3 m.
Kezia Withrow,	November 18, 1846,	47 y.
William J. Withrow,	December 12, 1846,	7 y.
Mary Ann Withrow,	December 25, 1846,	18 y.
Anna M. Wiley,	July 13, 1847,	1 y. 2 m. 10 d.
Louisa M. Wiley,	July 30, 1848,	5 y. 1 m. 15 d.

APPENDIX.

NAME.	DATE OF DEATH.	AGE.
Enoch Wallace,	July 16, 1850,	2 y. 4 m. 8 d.
John M. Withrow,	June 22, 1851,	48 y.
Sarah Withrow,	February 12, 1851,	66 y. 6 m. 12 d.
John Wiley,	May 27, 1852,	60 y.
Frances Withrow,	September 22, 1851,	24 y. 29 d.
Mary Jane Williams,	January 13, 1852,	29 y.
Elizabeth Withrow,	July 30, 1852,	83 y.
Hannah Williams,	May 31, 1853,	60 y.
Jeremiah Werntz,	April 6, 1854,	48 y.
J. Wilmer Wiley,	January 28, 1855,	1 y. 3 m. 26 d.
William Whiteside,	December 9, 1858,	60 y.
Charles W. Wright,	March 17, 1858,	10 m. 17 d.
Amanda Z. Walker,	February 6, 1860,	22 y. 3 m. 6 d.
Samuel S. Wilson,	May 12, 1860,	27 y.
Rebecca F. Wells,	October 2, 1861,	62 y.
Jane Whiteside,	April 10, 1863,	59 y.
John C. Walton,	June 16, 1868,	58 y. 11 m. 10 d.
Margaret Wright,	December, 1868,	25 y.
Margaret Whiteside,	July 30, 1869,	41 y.
Elizabeth D. Whiteside,	December 13, 1869,	39 y.
Thomas Wallace,	March 29, 1870,	77 y. 11 m.
Ann Wright,	October 5, 1870,	40 y. 10 m. 15 d.
Robert Wiley,	no date,	4 y.
Samuel Wright.		
Jane Wright.		
Vance Wright.		
Rachel Wilson,	October 25, 1870,	44 y. 2 m. 5 d.
Walter Andrew Young,	September 24, 1843,	8 m. 26 d.
John Parke Young,	September 4, 1854,	10 y. 5 m. 24 d.
Sallie Young,	August 17, 1861,	1 m. 28 d.
Matlack Young,	February 10, 1862,	52 y. 9 m. 12 d.

Abraham Kendig died June 4, 1864, aged 32 years, from wounds received in battle and was buried in the hospital burying-ground at Hampton, Virginia. He belonged to the 97th Reg't Penna. Volunteers, commanded by Colonel Guss.

Joseph Heslep Kendig died June 18, 1864, aged 22 years. He fell in battle before Petersburg, and rests in a soldier's grave on the battle field. He belonged to the 21st Penna. Cavalry, commanded by Col. Boyd.

L.

SURNAMES OF FAMILIES AND INDIVIDUALS COMPOSING THE UPPER OCTORARA CONGREGATION, 1870.

Armstrong,
Ash,
Andes,
Boyd,
Boggs,
Bent,
Best,
Bair,
Benson,
Blackburn,
Bonnar,
Brandt,
Boyle,
Bunting,
Brook,
Blankenbeler,
Cowan,
Clarke,
Carlile,
Chalfant,
Chapman,
Curry,
Cook,
Crawford,
Davis,
Dain,
Dean,
Dougal,
Duncan,
Delaine,
Drake,
Emerson,
Ferguson,
Fielis,
Filson,
Ferree,

Finney,
Fornwalt,
Frame,
Futhey,
Gibson,
Gayley,
Guthrie,
Graham,
Grossman,
Gable,
Hope,
Hoofman,
Holmes,
Hershberger,
Harley,
Houston,
Hawks,
Hudson,
Hinkson,
Himmens,
Irwin,
Ihler,
Jones,
Johnson,
Jack,
Jackson,
Jamison,
Kendig,
Kyle,
Keller,
Key,
Keats,
Long,
Latta,
Lincoln,
Linn,

Lewis,
MacGregor,
McPherson,
McClellan,
McAlister,
McCaughey,
McNaught,
McMichael,
McAloman,
Maitland,
Matlack,
Marsh,
Marshall,
Marple,
Mackey,
Martin,
Middleton,
Miller,
Moore,
Morris,
Murphey,
Mewes,
Orr,
Otty,
Owens,
Parke,
Parks,
Parker,
Paxson,
Pomeroy,
Potter,
Patrick,
Powers,
Pearl,
Pyle,
Phillips,

Ramsay,
Rawlins,
Rankin,
Reid,
Richmond,
Ross,
Stewart,
Sloan,
Scott,
Smith,
Shoemaker,
Shirk,
Strode,
Stroud,
Simpson,
Scholfield,
Skiles,
Taggart,
Thompson,
Todd,
Torbert,
Turner,
Vandersaal,
Varnes,
Valentine,
Wallace,
Walker,
Whiteside,
Wiley,
Wilson,
Williams,
Wike,
Worrest,
Yearsley,
Young.

www.ingramcontent.com/pod-product-compliance
Lightning Source LLC
Chambersburg PA
CBHW032136160426
43197CB00008B/670